A MILLER CENTER TENTH ANNIVERSARY
COMMEMORATIVE PUBLICATION 1975-1985

THE FORD
WHITE HOUSE

A Miller Center Conference
Chaired by Herbert J. Storing

Edited by

*The Staff of the White Burkett Miller Center
of Public Affairs at the University of Virginia*

UNIVERSITY
PRESS OF
AMERICA

LANHAM • NEW YORK • LONDON

Copyright © 1986 by

University Press of America,® Inc.

4720 Boston Way
Lanham, MD 20706

3 Henrietta Street
London WC2E 8LU England

Printed in the United States of America

Library of Congress Cataloging in Publication Data

The Ford White House : a Miller Center conference chaired
    by Herbert J. Storing.

    "A Miller Center tenth anniversary commemorative
publication 1975-1985."
    Based on conference discussions on the administration
of President Gerald R. Ford, held at the White Burkett
Miller Center of Public Affairs, on April 23, 1977.
    1. Presidents—United States—Staff—Congresses.
2. Ford, Gerald R., 1913-   Congresses.   3. United
States—Politics and government—1974-1977—Congresses.
I. Storing, Herbert J., 1928-   .   II. White Burkett
Miller Center.
JK518.F67   1986   353.03'1   86-1692
ISBN 0-8191-5301-X (alk.paper)
ISBN 0-8191-5302-8 (pbk. : alk. paper)

The views expressed by the author(s) of this publication do not necessarily represent
the opinions of the Miller Center. We hold to Jefferson's dictum that: "Truth is the
proper and sufficient antagonist to error, and has nothing to fear from the conflict,
unless, by human interposition, disarmed of her natural weapons, free argument and debate."

Co-published by arrangement with
The White Burkett Miller Center of Public Affairs,
University of Virginia

TABLE OF CONTENTS

ACKNOWLEDGEMENTS

It was Herbert Storing's idea to bring together a group of former advisers to President Gerald R. Ford for a candid discussion of their White House experiences in the spring of 1977. The conference took place before Professor Storing officially assumed his duties as Director of the Miller Center's Program on the Presidency and was hosted by Frederick Nolting, then the Director of the White Burkett Miller Center of Public Affairs.

The original transcript of the conference was edited by Joseph Bessette, with assistance from Gary Schmitt, and typed by Shirley Kingsbury. This version of the conference transcript was reviewed by all the Ford White House staff participants, edited and proofread by David Clinton, Blaire French, Lowell Gustafson, and Robert Strong. It was typed by Jacquelynn Harding.

PREFACE

On April 23, 1977, a conference on the administration of President Gerald R. Ford was held at the White Burkett Miller Center of Public Affairs. Under the chairmanship of the late Professor Herbert Storing, then the newly appointed Director of the Center's Program on the Presidency, a full day was devoted to informal conversation among key Ford White House staff members, associates of the Miller Center, and members of the University of Virginia community.

At that time there were no plans to publish the proceedings, which were intended to educate the conference participants—both scholars and practitioners—about the Ford presidency. In that regard the conference was extremely successful and is remembered by many participants as an unusually frank and serious discussion between those who have worked in the White House and those who have studied it.

During the next few years many of the people familiar with this project urged the Center to publish the Ford White House transcript as a tribute to Professor Storing, who died several months after the conference was held, and as a valuable document on the modern American presidency. As Herbert Storing's successor at the Miller Center, I got in touch with the conferees and asked their permission to publish the conference discussions. Each of the Ford Administration conferees was given the opportunity to review his statements in the transcript, and to make such corrections and editorial changes as were deemed appropriate. Three members of the Ford White House staff asked that their comments not be published; and their remarks, and references to them have been deleted from the transcript. Where such deletions have interrupted the flow of conversation, asterisks have been used to indicate a change in the subject under discussion. Several participants made minor editorial changes in their remarks which have been incorporated into this version. Others elected to leave their comments exactly as they were originally transcribed. Passages that were inaudible to the transcriber or speakers who could not be identified have been noted in the text.

In the short time he was associated with the Miller Center and in his long career as an educator and scholar, Herbert Storing made many friends and a lasting contribution to the study of American politics and the American presidency. This book is dedicated to his memory.

James Sterling Young

LIST OF PARTICIPANTS

Ford White House Staff

James H. Cavanaugh—deputy assistant to the President, 1976-1977; deputy assistant to the President for domestic affairs, 1974-1976.

Richard B. Cheney—White House chief of staff, 1975-1977; assistant to the President, 1975-1977; deputy assistant to the President, 1974-1975.

James E. Connor—secretary to the Cabinet, 1975-1977; staff secretary to the President, 1975-1977.

Robert A. Goldwin—special consultant to the President, 1974-1976; advisor to the secretary of defense, 1976.

James T. Lynn—director of the Office of Management and Budget, 1975-1977; secretary of housing and urban development, 1973-1975.

Donald H. Rumsfeld—assistant to the President and member of his Cabinet, 1974-1975; secretary of defense, 1975-1977.

Brent Scowcroft—assistant to the President for national security affairs, 1975-1977; deputy assistant to the President for national security affairs, 1973-1975.

Participants from the University of Virginia

Dennis W. Barnes
Frans R. Bax
Joseph M. Bessette
James W. Ceaser
Paul T. David
Laurin L. Henry
David C. Jordan

John B. Keeley
Frederick E. Nolting, Jr.
Steven E. Rhoads
David A. Shannon
Herbert Stein
Herbert J. Storing

FIRST SESSION

NOLTING: I want to welcome you on behalf of the University before turning the meeting over to our chairman, Mr. Storing, and particularly to welcome you to the new arm of the University as we call ourselves here at the Miller Center. The purpose of this meeting, as you know, the purpose of the Miller Center is to do what we are doing here, trying to combine in a mutually stimulating way scholastics' and practioners' thought—and many of you are both—and to develop this as a major center for the study of the presidency. I would like to say that I should think it would be a great satisfaction to you gentlemen who served in the Ford administration in the White House to get together again, because I imagine there was not too much time to do that sort of thing when you were on active duty. Certainly, in my opinion, I don't know of a group who did more to pull this country up by its bootstraps in a short time in terms of confidence and trust in the institutions of government and particularly in the Chief Executive's Office.

Herbert, the meeting is yours and please go right ahead.

STORING: Let me add my welcome, although I am only quasi-entitled to do so since I'm not really a permanent member of this University or this community yet, although I will be in July. I won't

1

take a lot of time, but I want to say a word about the program on the presidency of the Miller Center and about what I see our business here today being and something about the ground rules, which are negligible. The program on the presidency is so new it hardly yet exists and we are very much in the stage of thinking about what we want to do, and ought to do, and how, and the rest of it.

There are a couple of premises or principles that we're going to operate on. First of all, we are thinking of it in terms of a center for the scholarly study of the presidency. Our main business we do not expect to be to give advice to Presidents, although we'll do our share—every American citizen is entitled to think he knows what the President ought to do and we certainly will exercise that prerogative. But in the main we have it in mind to set up a center that will be a place for the serious scholarly study of the presidency. And, our particular concern, although not our exclusive concern, which, as a matter of fact, also reflects, I understand, the wishes of the founder of the Miller Center, is the broad question of the place of the President in our constitutional order. We'll read that quite widely and that will enable us to do just about anything we want to do. But it will mean that the sort of focus of our concern will be on that range of questions. The founder of the Miller Center, Burkett Miller, was, I understand, concerned with the sort of imperial presidency order of questions, and some of us will concern ourselves with that area. One of the early things I plan to do is a book on the creation of the presidency, the original design and intention of the presidency about which I think there is quite a bit of misunderstanding, about which there is no really satisfactory scholarly work. We plan a study on the impoundment controversy during the Nixon administration as a way of looking at the dynamics of the American system of checks and balances. We have in early stages a plan to do a study of the legislative veto which is also an area that, I think, has not been sufficiently studied. However, as I say, from that we will range out to a wide variety of things including the topic of our meeting today: the operation, organization, and management of the White House.

This is for me a kind of target of opportunity. It seemed to me that it would be useful before the Ford White House people settle completely into their private lives or to their other activities to see if we could get together some of them to meet with some of us here at the University of Virginia to talk informally about the lessons, if any, of their experience in the Ford White House. Bob Goldwin warned me that if we were going to do this we ought to do it fairly soon because many of the people from the White House would no doubt be talking formally and informally about their experience and if we didn't catch them soon they would soon be in a position where they couldn't distinguish between what they actually had done, and seen, and heard and what they *said* they had done, seen and heard. (Laughter) So we're trying to catch you before you've completely picked your position.

Now the conference here I see as a conversation among people of common interests for our mutual edification. The purpose is not to formulate rules for running the White House. The purpose is not to come up with a publication. The purpose is simply to try to help one another understand this topic of common interest. We are, as I have mentioned, and as you see, taping our conversation. And, as I've also said, the purpose of that is strictly educational, so that we can listen to it again if we want to, so that perhaps our students can do so. There will be no use made of the tapes in the way of publication without explicit permission from the pertinent parties.

Now I haven't got an agenda. That was my own judgment and it was also the universal judgment of all of you with whom I consulted. I don't think we could stick to it, and moreover one of the questions I think that we, that I, will find interesting is what the agenda should be, what questions we should be asking. I have, as you know, listed some questions that strike me as the kinds of questions that we want to at some point talk about. And if they don't come up naturally I will raise those questions, but I do not intend to confine us to that. And I am happy to entertain, and I know that at least some of you will propose, criticisms of the questions that I suggested or alternatives. And that's all to the good. I provided you with the (Stephen) Hess book on *Organizing the Presidency*, again, not for purposes of it providing us with an agenda, but because in the first place it seemed to me to provide quite useful case study background of the kinds of things that we are going to be interested in; and in the second place it strikes me as a pretty fair example of the sort of revisionist view of presidential management, and in that sense it's pertinent. The revisionist view may be described as a shift from the notion of the President as chief manager to the notion of a more collegial President or, more historically, a shift from the Jacksonian to the Whig view of the American presidency.

I do think we might keep in mind as we move through these discussions a broad scheme or direction which, it seems to me, might usefully run from the most particular things about the operation, and management and organization of the Ford White House, to more general questions. So that broadly it strikes me that those things that are most immediate and concrete and particular that we might want to talk about, it would be useful to talk about relatively early in the day and with the aim of moving toward the end of the day to the broader level, more general kinds of questions. Obviously, I don't expect that to be adhered to with any rigor, but I do think it might be useful if we kept that broad possibility in mind; and in the last hour I will try to make sure that everybody has an opportunity to deliver himself of whatever general reflections he might have as a result of our conversations. I think that we can proceed informally, without needing to be recognized by the chair and simply in the form of a conversation. I will try to guide the traffic and when it becomes necessary, if you give me a nod or something indicative that you have something you would like to say, I will keep a list and make it possible for the discussion to proceed in a moderately orderly fashion.

I would like to open the discusson by asking a question, directed, I suppose, in the first place to the people who were in the Ford White House, but not meant in any sense to be confined to them. What do you think are the things that were especially well done in the Ford White House, and what things, if any, were not so well done? Don, would you be willing to start us off?

RUMSFELD: Well, maybe the way to start is to just comment briefly on what I think it's probably accurate to say President Ford was *trying* to do. Then one can, I suppose, ask the question whether or not that's what he ought to have been trying to do and how well he did it. But the sense he had, and the sense that I think a number of the people in this room who were around him had, was that the problem he faced was one of trying to deal with basically two things at once. One was to provide a degree of continuity as the first President who wasn't elected and came in abruptly, and to see that the government ran, and that things worked this way. This was particularly important to foreign policy and national security affairs. And you can detect in the things he did a reflection of a concern that the United States be seen as a country where people had a reasonable idea which way they were going internationally and from the security standpoint.

At the same time, he recognized the need for change. There had *been* a change. There was a new President. There was a need in the country for something other than what had been, as a result of the resignation. There obviously was, he felt, a need for a sense of change because of the problems a President has leading and the fact that, for the preceding period, the preoccupation had been with Watergate, as opposed to governing. As the Ambassador (Nolting) indicated, the desire to do those things that might contribute, along with the most important ingredient of time, to restoring the Executive Office of the President to a position of sufficient respect and trust that a leader, who has to lead by persuasion and consent, is able to function. And, further, from a political standpoint, the elections that were associated with the Watergate period were not helpful to the Republican party. As a political leader, he had a desire to have sufficient change so that the prospects in the coming elections would hopefully be better. These are some of the things he was thinking about and the people around him were thinking about, trying to do during that period. And of course, that period was an important part of his administration, given the fact that it was a rather short one.

STORING: How did those concerns manifest themselves in operations, or organization, or behavior?

RUMSFELD: Just one example, one of the first things he did—in fact I was not in the country, but it is my recollection—even before he was sworn in, he indicated his support for Henry Kissinger, his desire to have the world understand that he knew they were in general agreement, that he was going to stay and that the rest of the world could rely on a degree of continuity from the standpoint of foreign policy. I don't remember when he did it, but he had done it by the time I was back in the United States.

SCOWCROFT: One of his very first acts on Inauguration Day was to call in the ambassadors of virtually every country with whom we had substantial relations and talk to them. He spent a good part of the first day doing that, in batches for some, singularly with others.

GOLDWIN: And then when there was a lot of talk about separating the positions of secretary of state and national security advisor—both of which Kissinger held. The President inserted a paragraph in his speech to the U.N. General Assembly, that Kissinger would continue in both posts. That was little more than a month after President Ford assumed office. So a concern must have persisted about the continuity of our foreign policy, and President Ford was still talking about it, trying to give assurances in as public and formal a way as possible.

RUMSFELD: If you took the two things, continuity and the desire for a sense of some change, you could say the former weighed heavier on the earlier period of his administration and the latter weighed heavier on him during the latter portion of his administration.

NOLTING: Could I ask, Mr. Chairman, when you spoke of calling the ambassadors—I suppose mostly the NATO ambassadors and people of that sort...

SCOWCROFT: It was NATO, Latin America, Africa, Asia ... pretty much everybody.

NOLTING: Everybody! Was there much malaise felt by them at the time? I was trying to get at the point of whether or not this transition was one that was particularly difficult from the point of view of foreign policy.

RUMSFELD: I couldn't answer it from the standpoint of the White House—I was in Brussels. From *that* standpoint there is no question but that the people I was dealing with from those fourteen other countries were pro-Nixon, admired him, were supportive of him, could not understand what in the world the United States was doing to itself, and didn't know Vice-President Ford. Change is uncomfortable to begin with, but when you are losing someone you admire, and feel a relationship with, to an unknown, it is disturbing. And there is no question that, at least as far as NATO countries were concerned, there was a need for someone to reach out and communicate with them and touch them and let them know how they were going to get back in that place and link up.

CHENEY: Maybe the key point here in terms of the transition, I can't overemphasize strongly enough in my own mind how important it is to separate out that kind of transition from even though it's within one party, Republican–Republican—it was unique respective to Kennedy to Johnson or someone else. Whereas LBJ was perfectly free when he took over, and indeed all of the external pressures so to speak on him were to stress continuity, that he'd ask everybody to continue, and that to some extent his own political future in 1964 depended upon the ability of him to identify with his predecessor. We had exactly the opposite situation. Although there was great pressure for continuity in foreign policy there was much greater pressure—not relative to the pressure for continuity, but greater pressure relative to what a new President ordinarily finds coming into office in that fashion—for *change*: to be able to persuade the American people that we had significantly modified and altered the way of doing business in the White House, who the key people were, made some changes in the cabinet and so forth, the kinds of pressures that LBJ, for example, never had to face. And I think it was a factor for two and one half years, all the time we were there.

*   *   *

SCROWCROFT: There's another element to the 25th amendment, and that is the character of events which led to it. In many respects, you know, the transition was not that different in the fact of a new President assuming office in a very sudden manner to the Kennedy-Johnson. Circumstances were very different. The assassination of Kennedy brought the country together. There was an enormous outwelling of support and national unity. Quite the converse was true when President Ford took over. He took over in circumstances of deep division within the country and the circumstances of the resignation led him to take an act very shortly thereafter, the pardon, to deal with those circumstances which I think pretty nearly ended the traditional honeymoon of the new President, in giving him time; because, you know, this mobilized the press and it focused attention on him and in a critical way which didn't happen with Johnson.

CHENEY: It makes a big difference whether you bury your predecessor or your partner. (Laughter) That shouldn't be overlooked.

CEASER: I was wondering, the two elements that Mr. Rumsfeld mentioned of continuity and change, they're both objectives but they are also, I think, perceived by the American people as somewhat in tension. Because the elements of continuity, while it was important for the allies, also involved the maintenance of Kissinger's power in the form which was, I think, associated with Nixon's type of White House.

And I wondered in the early stages whether there was some balance made, a balance sought between the desire of the country to change the form of executive organization and the need of foreign powers to see continuity in our policy.

CHENEY: Maybe, for those who weren't part of the Ford White House, it would be helpful to be very basic in describing ... answering Jim's question, the concept that we tried to pursue—Don helped design the system the President was interested in, we talked about the transition period—it´ was the idea that the President ought to have multiple sources of information. But that when it came time to make a decision there was only one channel to proceed through. And that channel, basically, was for National Security Council, or Domestic Council, or OMB to do an options paper with everybody that ought to be consulted on it. It was seen to that they were consulted on it in terms of their views being presented; that the pros and cons be argued vigorously; that a fairly standard format be used in terms of presenting that information to the President; and that he never got blindsided by having a decision going to him around the system in such a way that he didn't have all those other sources of information when it came time for him to make the call. I think the key point is that in a case like common situs picketing—we got in trouble because we didn't adhere to that fundamental procedure.

STEIN: I must explain I only had twenty-one days in the Ford White House and I cannot speak very well about it, but I think there were certain similarities and I think this description of the system that you have given is a rather formal one, that really the system operated quite differently in different areas. I think of it as being three systems. I think there's the foreign affairs system which most of the time was a one on one, the President and one other, and there wasn't all this business, a lot of clearing around. I mean the department of agriculture never did (inaudible) and neither did hardly anybody else.

RUMSFELD: You're talking about the Nixon White House, aren't you?

STEIN: Yes, I'm not sure that I'm talking about the Ford White House but I am talking about the Nixon White House.

SCOWCROFT: Not to the same extent.

STEIN: I think it's different in degree, that area is different in degree. I think that the economic area was an area kind of self-contained, say Treasury, OMB, CEA, the Cost of Living Council. When we had that apparatus, the White House staff did not clear option papers. They never injected themselves very much. Even in what somebody called those imperial days, Haldeman never said a thing about that. Then there are all those outlying fellows HUD and HEW and so on, and they are the people who are the main objects of this system of paper clearance and options preparation, by specifically White House staff.

LYNN: You asked initially the question what did we do well and what was the bad side of what we did. Let's get away from the political apparatus and so on, because I'm not a politician. I'll let the politicians talk about that. (Laughter) But on the actual running of the White House, I would say the good was, I think, on refinement or maybe a return to old systems, because I don't have that sense of history, of policy formulation and the decisonmaking process. You can say, that it was the same system. I would say to you from the perspective of having been a cabinet member at HUD in the Nixon years, and before that, in the subcabinet, and what I saw in the Ford White House, there were *tremendous* differences. Let me explain them from the perspective of someone who saw both. Yes, there was in both administrations a process for the paper to come in to the President, but there were two very great differences. One was, as Dick was saying, that in the Ford administration there was a concerted effort made to be sure that the views of competing missions, I might say, amongst departments, amongst staff people, and otherwise, were put together all in one place, in one paper. And everybody knew how the other person's position was stated. Now that might not seem very important, but I can tell you as secretary of HUD in the old days one of the things that used to drive me nuts was that on an appeal, let's say on the budget, if I wanted to appeal a budget decision I wrote up an appeal paper in my own form—they let me write it any way I wanted it and any length I wanted it—to the President. Then OMB would write a response. They saw my paper. I didn't see theirs. It was like an appeal court where one lawyer sees the other lawyer's brief and writes then his brief which the first lawyer never sees. Then it went into the President with the OMB paper on top—no, excuse me, some staff member's paper went even on top of the OMB paper. And unless the President feels like a tiger and is totally absorbed by the subject matter—and I can tell you he wouldn't be on Section 235 Housing—he's going to read the top little paper which the cabinet officer never saw, he might read the OMB paper which the cabinet officer never saw, and if he ever got to any part of the cabinet officer's paper it was a miracle.

Let's get down to it; there were fundamental differences. Now these are not things that will impress the American people at large. They tend to create, however, an impression amongst the career people who are out in the agencies. It creates a somewhat different impression to the press, the media—I mean the media that works constantly with the White House and with the executive branch of the government. And to some extent, a lesser extent, it affects attitudes to accept things that come hard. But I am saying to you, as a way of doing business, when President Ford came in, we for example in OMB for the first time when there was a budget appeal, a joint paper was written which the department had worked on with OMB, and knew exactly what was stated. If there was a disagreement on facts, as the background on the domestic side, or in defense, or whatever it was to be, the disagreement was stated right on the face of it, that there is a factual disagreement, and that we don't have the time or we don't know *how* to get an answer to that fact or semi-fact. The pros and cons were stated. If someone didn't believe it was a con, it was stated, "X doesn't really believe this is a con and here is why" as opposed to a pro. Then, most important of all, there was almost always an opportunity for a followup—head-to-head discussion of the matter with the President. In fact, seeing the President's evolution on how he wanted to do business was one of the most intriguing things. Richard Nixon wanted the written word, that's well known. He didn't want the oral. Gerald Ford came in and the first three days he was in office he said to many different people, "Now I'm a person who likes to just get a bunch of people around a table and have it out head-to-head with them." If you heard him in the first few days a paper would be meaningless. However, it wasn't three weeks later that I was in a meeting with him and he was growling because he hadn't had the paper first. And what he evolved was the best of the systems, which is to get the combination of the well-prepared paper which everyone has had an opportunity to see, comment, and refine and then have the head-to-head discussion where the President can really get the feel for things that a person is not willing to put in a paper. Because, let's face it, in a political world and in a world of leaks and in a world where not everyone can get the exact nuance in a writing of what their position really is, a head-to-head discussion gives the President an opportunity to verify various positions of the players, to sniff out the nuances and the tradeoffs. Now this was a fundamental difference between those White Houses.

STORING: I just want to say, why do you think that change occurred? You said—I know you want to pursue the question of whether there was a difference but leaving that aside—from what you said I can see two possible reasons. One would be, one might have to do with your own experience under the Nixon administration, and I was interested in knowing whether it was Ford's initiative that caused this new system, Jim? What was the reason for this, as you described, quite significant...

LYNN: Multiple reasons. First of all there was the feeling that has already been expressed that the Nixon White House was a very tight closed-in place where one or two people were running the whole thing, and one reason was to create a change. Remember, we were looking for different ways of doing things. And this was a very different way that would impact on public perception. So it was done from that perspective. It was done secondly because Gerald Ford, as a human being, had a sense of fairness. It was done thirdly in my judgment because, I think, President Ford based on his Hill experience, had learned that you're very well advised to touch all the bases. Now, somebody once described politics as like baseball. All you've got to do is touch all the bases. But as one old-timer told me when I first came into government, there are two fundamental differences: one is there are a hell of a lot more bases than three or four, and secondly their geographic location is constantly changing. And if you come at it with that viewpoint you then want, if you're sitting in the White House, not to be blindsided; in the head-to-head you may get some nuance, either political or substantive, that you won't otherwise get. And from the standpoint also of good sound policymaking you want multiple views. But it's all those elements combined and probably others.

CHENEY: But in reference to Herb's (Storing) question wouldn't everybody agree that the dominant factor was the President?

LYNN: Absolutely.

CONNOR: Maybe for some of the people here it might make sense to put the description of the system in context. What it *wasn't*, and what it consciously wasn't was a Roosevelt system: finding different people, giving them responsibilities or charges, which would overlap, letting them compete, letting them build their cases, and then letting the President make the decision.

And using the departments as well as White House staff and setting them off against each other—a very conscious effort was made to avoid that. An effort in a sense not to throw seeds out and see which ones grow, but rather to sit on top of the process, order it, keep things from popping out that you don't know about, that you don't have an ability to understand all the implications of. It's a very conservative kind of a system. I am much more concerned about the things the government is going to pop up with than I am about the good idea that will pop here, there, and elsewhere if I put people in competition. The approach in the Ford White House, it seems to me, was one designed to slow down the process, to keep things from popping out, slow it down and order it, as much as you can in order to understand what the implications for a presidential decision are, rather than saying, "If I set enough interesting things in motion some interesting things will arise." And I think this whole system designed under Eisenhower and carried through under Nixon and Ford, even given the differences of how each man did it, was really set for that purpose; to get a control over the government.

CEASER: The staff people probably see things in terms of personality whereas a political scientist on the outside can only see things in terms of institutions. And the feeling expressed here is that the change between Nixon and Ford was one of personality. But from our point of view maybe it was more, to a greater extent, a change in institution. Mr. Lynn mentioned, in addition to Ford's personality, he mentioned the fact that he felt the process was too tight-fisted under Nixon. I think looking from the outside you can see it building up within the country and maybe in President Ford's mind a feeling that the staff was too powerful vis-a-vis the cabinet. And that this greater access of cabinet members was not simply a change in personality but represented a slight institutional change.

LYNN: Let me give you an anecdote on that that is kind of interesting. I remember when I first became OMB director the press was very anxious to know whether I had read the transitional paper on OMB, and what OMB was and what it ought to be, and why was I made OMB director. And on the last question I say, it beats me. Maybe they wanted to punish me somehow—a strong form of purgatory— although it's probably the second most interesting job in the federal government. But on the first part I would always say to the press, no, I haven't asked to see it. And the President really never gave me any directions in the sense of telling me what was in that paper or what I ought to do in that job. But I think he knew from my own style of doing things that he was going to get what he wanted, which was not only an impression of fairness but loosening up that system in the sense of being sure that those options were presented to him in the right way. He was going to find more consultation because he knew I was a Hill type, that I like the Hill, that I liked going up there and talking to people before we said no. And it makes a big difference as to whether you go up and talk to them and they understand why it is you are saying no, if you have to say no and so on. But my point in that regard is he was very, I think, careful in how he went about these appointments in the sense of not giving a direction, not saying, "This is exactly what I want to have by way of an impression or a creation." But as he chose the people he had that very much in mind, that he wasn't going to change their spots, but he was looking for people with the spots that he liked.

CHENEY: Something Jim mentioned here that the staff was too powerful I don't think ought to be permitted.

LYNN: I didn't say "tight-fisted," I don't remember using that word.

CHENEY: Well, just aside from that, part of the revisionist history you mentioned at the outset, the revisionist view of the White House ...

STORING: Not mine, I ...

CHENEY: The concept I think that we responded to a little bit, the Carter people have overreacted to some extent, and I think that it is sort of fashionable to talk about, to look at the Nixon White House and look at characteristics like quote "powerful staff members" or a tight structured organization and conclude that that was the cause of Watergate. And in going through that whole process you then make judgments like the staff was too powerful, and that that was a problem. I don't think we ought to fall into the trap—I would argue anyway giving my own views—of making the same kinds of mistakes that perhaps we made at the very outset of the Ford administration, and that I think, for example, Carter has made, and I think Hess makes in his book in terms of letting the organization of the Nixon White House and Watergate lead you to some value judgments about how the White House should be organized.

STORING: Let me just make a distinction that we ought to keep in mind as we go on. I think that's a good point but I think it's also true that there is also an argument which you sée in Hess in a sometimes vague way that there's a defect or a danger in this growth of staff, White House staff, that's independent of Watergate altogether. I mean there is surely a respectable argument to the effect that there is something wrong with modern American government and that is is connected with the accumulation of lots of power in the White House office which has various bad consquences, one of which is—well, it may not be *true*, all I'm for the present arguing is that one doesn't have to associate this whole thing with Watergate in order to make an argument that needs to be taken up. That's my only point.

*   *   *

SCOWCROFT: I would like to address a point about that personality vs. structure. The structure was maintained thoroughly, thoroughly (inaudible), and the principal difference was personality. Both President Nixon and Bob Haldeman were more formidable people personally. They were not open and warm in the sense of accessibility. And one thought very seriously before you asked to go in and get a decision reversed. Because the cabinet officers and the staff members knew that if you went in there frivolously there were going to be problems and penalties down the road. That was not true with President Ford. The result was that the process tended to not only open up but be treated a little more cavalierly because the people knew they would always have another word, that they would send the paper in, fine, and if they got their way, fine, and if they didn't they would always have another shot at it.

STORING: Might that not lead—I'm thinking of Rumsfeld's rules, one of which is be precise, I think, or some such thing—might that not lead to looseness of thinking and carelessness? Could a substantial argument be made to the effect that the Ford system does in fact tend to blunt sharp thinking and loosen up understanding of alternatives and make the whole thing rather more amorphous?

LYNN: That depends, it seems to me, on the people that are in this structure, the Eisenhower structures; it depends on how much a President and those staff heads, whatever names they put on them, impose discipline in that regard. And let's bear in mind that this administration was two and one-half years. Let's bear in mind that during the first few months it was being kicked off the end of the pier and somebody saying swim, darn you. Then comes an election, a congressional election fast upon that. Then there was a breather period of maybe eight months where you really had a relative freedom to govern. By that I mean where the political pressures of the upcoming presidential election were not yet enormous. Now comes an election year for the whole last six, eight, ten months.

In a normal four-year term you've got a stand of eighteen months in there where you are relatively free of that. But having been through two administrations and looking at the quality of papers and the numbers of papers and the degree of attention to them, that there is a direct correlation with the number of months that you are away from or getting close to November, whatever the Tuesday date is. And, therefore, for us to talk about how there may have been some disintegration of the paperwork, that perhaps there wasn't the care and discipline with regard to it, let's put that in a context that at least during the last six to eight months all of us had feelings both for running the government but also for getting Gerald Ford elected because we felt very strongly about that. And that takes away time of those cabinet officers who would normally be spending more time looking at that paper. They say, "The heck with it, I'm going to do thus and such which I consider is important to a continuance of four more years of good government, and I'll wait until I get into that meeting with the

President to get my two bits in on an *ad hoc* basis." And you tell me which is the higher priority at that point. I might make a pretty good argument that what they did is of a higher priority.

But there is also another thing that you shouldn't ignore. There's a natural phenomenon with a cabinet officer. Its' this: given the time constraints on a cabinet officer's time, the competing demands for his time, given his own areas or her own areas of interests, and so on, cabinet officers many times would read the paper and think it was a good paper because they really hadn't participated themselves in their own department's preparation of the paper, and between the time of the preparation of the paper when they had seen the competing viewpoints put in that paper and the oral meeting they get up to speed. And many times—it was a crash job of getting up to speed—they would come in with an entirely different idea than they had at the time of the paper because they took that opportunity *between* the paper and the meeting, because they didn't want to look stupid in front of the President and finally did their homework between the paper and the meeting. And that was part of it. I could name names, but there are a number of cases where that was true. The cabinet office had been out on the road at the time when the paper was prepared. He wasn't there. So an assistant had helped prepare the paper, or a deputy to an assistant secretary really had done the paper. And then when the secretary got back and was going to have to go to the meeting where that was to be discussed, he would then suddenly assemble all his troops out there and do the job.

And I'll use this opportunity—you said what was the *worst* part or what we didn't do well, and this is where you get over to the Hess type of problem, is on the follow up. The decisionmaking process on the whole, the formulation of policy on the whole, I think, was reasonably well done, given all of the constraints and difficulties. But the follow through, to see that the policies and programs were carried out, was not well done. Perhaps the system to do it was satisfactory, but the makeup of the cabinet officers and what they sensed as their sense of priorities was such that you didn't get, as Hess would call it, the second and third effort toward the carrying out of those policies and decisions. Now again, part of our problem was in having only two and one-half years and with the constraints on cabinet selection. What no chief executive has done in fifty years is freely fire cabinet officers that don't keep to your sense of priorities. When you get to within the eight to ten months of an election you have to do that extremely sparingly. Who's going to come in for ten months? Who's going to learn the job in the ten months? But if I were to point out the one single factor that I found we didn't do well, and I've got some good excuses as they say—the shorter period of time, coming election, and all of the aroma and environment that we came into—we did *not* do the follow up to policy determination well. I'd have to say that in the Nixon first four years that was not done well. One of the tragedies of Watergate from a public administration standpoint is, I think, Richard Nixon had learned a good deal about that in the first four years, and had had some ideas with regard to what to do with the second four years, and he lost his power to do it as Watergate eroded that power.

CHENEY: The difference between formulation and implementation (inaudible) is the function of the beast. That is to say, it's a lot more exciting to go to the Oval Office and (inaudible) about world affairs to make a decision than it is to go back and try to get the bureaucracy to respond.

LYNN: Or to go to the Hill for the umpteenth time for the next six months, to have bourbon or brandy or Coca-Cola to convince them that what you are doing makes sense.

CHENEY: There are no awards for that.

NOLTING: A point has been touched on, maybe a little more elaboration would help on it. What puzzles me is two things: the time factor, and let's just talk about the President for the time being, and the energy quotient. I gather than President Nixon spent less time through his method of operating on these decisions, on each decision we'll say, than President Ford did, because he didn't want to give and take. Now, how far can that go, and could you make any comparisons, we'll say, between the number of hours worked each day of the week by the two Presidents?

RUMSFELD: It seems to me your original premise might be wrong. I didn't have the same perspective in the two administrations but my impression is that Mr. Nixon made fewer decisions than Ford did. That is to say, Mr. Nixon delegated more. It's not clear to me that he spent less time on decisions, that is to say, if you're doing fewer you may spend *more* time in terms of the numbers of hours worked, which is a separable issue. It seems to me that for both of them it was pretty much their life. If motion is work, one would have to say that Mr. Ford worked harder, goodness knows, than a horse. I mean he worked all the time, and read, and was physically around, available. Nixon was more remote, but whether that means he wasn't working as hard is not clear to me.

NOLTING: Take the case of the person who is constantly available and works eighteen hours, or whatever it is, to get his desk cleared for that day.

RUMSFELD: Is that what you mean by work?

NOLTING: Well, does he have the time to sit back?

RUMSFELD: Yes, President Ford had as much or more time than he wanted to sit back. He didn't. In other words, how much is enough? It varies with the human being.

NOLTING: I see.

CHENEY: But he changed over time, though. I think that would be, (inaudible). Look on the scheduling experience of a two and one-half year period of time. At the outset he would see virtually anybody. Later on he was more discriminating in the use of this time, perhaps. There were fewer meetings that went on endlessly and we ended up scheduling meetings on an as-needed basis rather than guaranteeing that every day somebody was going to be in there. He was going to be in there if he needs to see him. But it's not on a guaranteed basis.

STEIN: I think the question that was raised about time is very important. That is, there are going to be an awful lot of issues in the government that involve more than one agency. Those are the kinds of issues that come to the executive office. And you have to decide how many of those are the President's business; and if they're not the President's business whose are they? And if they're not the President's business then they are the business of some kind of machinery in the White House for either getting, either opposing a decision or reaching a collective decision. And I think, again, this is a matter in which

Presidents operate differently in different fields. I think that what Don (Rumsfeld) is saying is that at least in a lot of fields, probably excluding foreign affairs, President Nixon had the machinery for handling these decisions which didn't involve them coming to him. And that may be what looks like the imposition of the power of the White House, but it is also a way of concentrating the attention of the President on what are key issues.

I think there is another thing to say about this written vs. oral business. It's always perplexed me some. There is a general feeling that the decisions are better made if there are oral presentations. But I have a feeling, maybe from the brief life of John Connally, that it's better if everybody write a paper than if everybody gets in a room together with the President. John will always win if he's in a room with the President. (Laughter) But if everybody writes a paper he has a fighting chance. The point is that there is a power of personality over logic which you have to guard against or at least balance off by a certain amount of dry paperwriting. Of course paperwriting can be more or less persuasive, but tricky also.

*   *   *

LYNN: We were apt to treat an issue as a decision package that's fairly small without starting with the overall concept and working down to that decision. We were too apt to have not framed a principle, and then work our decisions within those principles. Now, I say two things about that: a) it was true. And I think Brent (Scowcroft) would agree with me that in national security, Brent and I had quite a struggle and we got joined by Rummy (Rumsfeld) and others finally in getting an overall concept and working from concepts down to specifics in those areas, toward the very end. But part of it was due to the time pressures of never having had that eighteen months that I talked about relatively in a four year term where there is almost a luxury period, you'd say. Another reason I would say, to be frank about it is, that President Ford had spent twenty-five years in an atmosphere where your function and your performance in that function is a series of quick decisionmaking in small concrete areas—I mean small compared to an overall concept. There is going to be a vote, yes or no. There is a bill and it's got so many lines in it and you're going to vote, yes or no. And where do you get the votes, either to pass it or defeat it. And what I saw—again one of my own personal senses of tragedy in his not continuing for a second term is that as he was in that office, at first it came hard to get him to conceptualize, to start with a broader principle and come down to considering a specific problem within the context of a principle. But toward the end of the term he was taking to that much better than he had in the beginning. And he had learned the importance of doing it that way, that everything, to use Moynihan, is related to everything else; and why is it that we have matching programs in this area and we don't require a match in another; why on some welfare programs are they geographically variable to reflect cost of living in different parts of the country but on social security it's a uniform amount no matter where you live; and on and on. In defense, starting with research and what is going to be the state of technology in 1985 or 1990 when the ships are going to come out and working back to your explicit decisionmaking in that mode. But, as I say, I think we didn't have as much of that conceptualizing as I would have liked at least, and I think there are good reasons for it. But there's got to be, in my judgment, the mechanism . . . well, let's back up. The mechanism, I think, afforded the opportunity for that. There isn't any doubt of it. There were mechanisms on the books—Senior Review Group mechanisms, the NSC review groups, and so on. But they had fallen into disuse, let's face it, over a period of time. I think there were a series of occupants in various jobs where "who needed that?" was the attitude. It was in the Ford administration that the rust was starting to come off of them, and it gave rise to some good *hoe-down* type battles, as more views were presented. But they were *starting* to come back. I'd have to say "starting," because they weren't fully working again, I think it's fair to say, by November two of last year.

*   *   *

CHENEY: You obviously have to consider the time and the problems we had to work under. But I felt that most of the President's time ultimately was allocated to things where external factors with a normal cycle in Washington, the budget cycle, the State of the Union address, etc. And in terms of really being able to hold back resources and allocate them to something that you wanted to have considered that hadn't previously been considered, it was very very difficult.

SCOWCROFT: I don't think, again, we ought to underemphasize the importance of personality in this whole thing. President Ford was action oriented. It was his whole career, that way. It was the way he was personally. He liked to get into things; he liked to look at papers; he liked to make decisions.

RUMSFELD: He really *did* like to make decisions.

SCOWCROFT: And one of the ways he arrived at decisions was meeting and having people bounce ideas back and forth. That's the way he got to his decisions. And President Nixon did it very differently. He liked to get the papers and he liked to squirrel himself away and think about them, or however he did it, because he did it by himself. Now, you can say one is better or one is worse, but the purpose of this whole process that we're describing here is to help the President make the best possible decisions and in doing that you have to direct yourself to the personality of the man.

CONNOR: Just to follow up on that, I think it's very clear that a President gets the decisionmaking system he's comfortable with. And if he's not comfortable with it—Don (Rumsfeld) can give examples and I think anybody that's ever been around any President can give examples—that a President can convey very clearly when he doesn't like somebody's nice suggestion for doing things. He has the power to do that.

RUMSFELD: For the reasons that have been mentioned and some others, there's some danger in this discussion that we are comparing Nixon at the end of his term to Ford at the beginning of his term.

SCOWCROFT: That's a good point.

RUMSFELD: Take them both. Ask yourself how Mr. Nixon interacted with his budget director in 1969. Compare it with how Gerald Ford interacted—compare it with how Gerald Ford interacted with Jim Lynn in 1974 and 1975. It's very different. President Ford had a long background in budget matters and was interested in it . . .

LYNN: He also knew that it was the one chance that you had every year to take a look at the whole scheme of things that have any kind of money implication—and what doesn't have such implication?

RUMSFELD: So he jumped in with both feet. He also, as we've said, was a congressman. He was used to reacting, to dealing with a lot of different subjects in a given hour's period on the floor of the House of Representatives, massaging people. He enjoyed it, was familiar with it, comfortable with it. Also, you've got to remember, he was getting good press for doing things the way he was doing them. In other words, there was a reward that was out there, the fact that he was doing things differently as an antidote to what was. Quite apart from whether it was effective, quite apart from whether it was sensible, quite apart from whether it was producing good policy, he was getting a daily reward—not an irrelevant consideration, it seems to me. When I think about that big question you asked at the beginning, you know, what did you do well, what didn't you do so well, maybe it's a bias, but when you think: he wasn't elected vice-president; he wasn't elected President; blew a major fraction of the goodwill that existed with the pardon; and with a major misstep as a result of the economic summit where everyone came in and was agreed that something was right that was wrong in October of 1974; yet generally with the economy, pretty good; generally with foreign policy and national security, pretty good; generally with budget directions and domestic directions, not a bad record; and came within a small margin of getting reelected, in terms of a public measurement, which is also not an irrelevancy.

CAVANAUGH: Well, I was kind of, Herb just made the point that Don (Rumsfeld) then went ahead and made, that we were comparing the end of the Nixon presidency with two and one-half years of the Ford presidency perhaps more than we should be. And then getting back to a question that Jim (Ceaser) raised earlier about differences in personality vs. the institution of the presidency, and I'd like to believe my observation on the Ford presidency that, yes, his personality was different, was much more open—he was a creature of the Congress, he was a congressman not an attorney—but that he brought to the presidency, I think, a different institutional view of the role of the President than we had seen during the Nixon years in terms of the role of the Congress in shaping policy and the role of the cabinet in shaping policy. And I think that was evidenced by the amount of time that he was willing to spend with congressmen, with chairmen of the committees, and with members of the cabinet that he had nominated on the business of the government. And so I think—although, sure, there were personality differences and sure, he enjoyed meetings and enjoyed seeing people—I do think he brought a little different institutional perspective to the Oval Office about Congress and about the cabinet.

*   *   *

CONNOR: It is my recollection that in a great many cases the paper that went up to the President finally didn't have a single recommended decision; they had different people recommending different kinds of decisions. And the whole purpose of the staffing exercise was to make very sure that everybody got a chance to say what it was they wanted to recommend. Now some of the different recommendations were predictable and sometimes you could soften the differences, but not all papers went up to the President with everybody recommending option A.

I don't recollect that the senior White House staff usually agreed on a single recommendation. One would come in one way and somebody else come in another, and then what you have are packages of opinions. The counsel's office would stress one thing and the people with congressional perspective would stress another. The whole purpose of the exercise, from my position, was to flesh it out, to show that there were different perspectives on decisions and to ensure that the President knew what they were.

*   *   *

RUMSFELD: If you take the basic question we're talking about here, it may or may not be of interest, but it is interesting to me, the President personally addressed it, thought about it in the very first week, discussed it, discussed it, discussed it. The theory was, as I recall the discussion, it was that you gain something and you give up something. You gain it by seeing that something is tested in a small marketplace. You gain the advantage of getting other people's ideas and you may improve the policy decision. You gain the fact that you will tend to have more people on board and supportive of what it is you are doing if they've been consulted. You gain the fact that those people who you have appointed will not be embarrassed by not knowing what it was you were doing, and therefore either resign or have bad morale or start feeling out of the action. You lose something also. You lost speed and you lost secrecy. You couldn't have done the China bit through the staff system. By doing it the way it was done, Secretary of State Bill Rogers looked like he was out of action. Now, the point that we talked about with President Ford was: know that there are those two different ways to do it. Know that you are going to gain something and lose something either way you go.

STORING: State what the two different ways are.

RUMSFELD: One way is to take a subject that you want to address and want to do something on and make a conscious decision that you are going to engage the people who have useful advice and counsel on that subject and/or who have a statutory responsibility in that area or a political responsibility in that area, and see that they are part of that decisionmaking process because you feel that the things to be gained by using that approach are greater than what you give up, in terms of losing speed and secrecy.

NOLTING: Whether or not it becomes a part of public, whether or not it leaks.

RUMSFELD: Right. Or you make a conscious decision as you would with the case on China, that you're not going to do that. Now, all I ever said to the President was: know which one you're using in a given area and make sure you consider the risks before you do it. Now it happens, you know, from a personal standpoint that I tended to feel as a human being a little more comfortable with a little more order and a little more discipline. He tended to believe that the spokes of the wheel would work, that he could be the integrator, the coordinator, as those threads come in from widely different places, and personnally see that there was a proper meshing. But that's a matter of personal per-ference.

STORING: Yes, it is, although it's also a characteristic difference between number one and number two. Number one tends to think that he can do it and number two tends to think that he needs (inaudible).

RUMSFELD: One last thought. The other thing that bothers me a bit about the discussion is, that if you take the opening comments on continuity and change, it reminds me a little bit of when I went over to take over OEO. The goal there was on action and innovation. Now you can have action or innovation, something that's bold, new and innovative, that's stupid. At some point you have to go to the measure of effectiveness. And continuity and change did not come out of the air as a goal. They were premised in his mind on his effectiveness as President. But the test ought to be effectiveness; the test ought *not* to be—is this change or is this continuity? It has to be effective. And there is always the danger that people end up chasing the wrong thing.

GOLDWIN: What I wanted to say before, Don (Rumsfeld), was really just a question for you. There is a part we've been passing over, and I think if you would discuss it at some length it would put a lot of these tensions we've been talking about in a better perspective. You didn't come into the White House in August, but when was it?

RUMSFELD: Early October, I believe, on a full-time basis.

GOLDWIN: And a lot had happened . . .

RUMSFELD: I was there for eleven days.

GOLDWIN: There was, one might say, a felt need to have Don in the White House, because of certain things that began to develop that were themselves very much a part of Ford's way of operating, and his hopes for what the presidency would be like, that were then causing him a lot of trouble. And so there was a desire to have Rumsfeld in the White House because he was going to do things differently. And if you could talk about what had happened up to the time you came to the White House and what you then saw had to be done—directed, regularized, and institutionalized and so on—I think that would throw a lot of light on these other tensions we've been talking about: personality and institutions, openness and precision, written and oral alternatives for decisions, and all the other things you had to deal with.

RUMSFELD: Oh, golly, I don't know that I'm the best one to talk about it, but it seems to me that there were—I was there as I recall for ten or twelve days during the transition, and we made a judgment that that transition team ought to probably be different from any other transition team because every other transition team moves in and takes over the government. And you had a choice: either you did that, or you developed a self-destruct on the transition team. We decided very early on that the President's tilt towards continuity made the idea of having the transition team continue to a position of assuming the government fundamentally unwise. So the very afternoon I arrived in town we suggested to the President that we would set an outside limit of three to four weeks on the existence of the transition team. We talked with the members, and the President agreed. It turned out we ended up only twelve days, I think, but hopefully with some ways that he could intervene to see that the transition continued because he also knew he had to have some change.

When I came back I'd never seen such a change in the environment in my entire life, 80% as a result of the pardon. Everything was different. Furthermore, a lot of decisions had been made. And, third, there was a pressure on the part of some elements in the government, particularly the press as part of that environment, to have more change faster. And Al Haig, who obviously was perfectly capable of doing the job that the President had asked him to do, that is to say, he in that principal post during the duration of his term, what I recall was the understanding, at least for the foreseeable future. Al felt and the President agreed that he was really falling prey to that pressure for immediate change that the press was putting on and some people in the government were putting on.

The other thing of note was a feeling that absent a change in that sort there was a likelihood that the degree of disorder that had evolved during that period would probably continue and accentuate because of the strong feelings that there ought to be a change. That is to say, there may have been an unwillingness for some Ford people to place their ideas, their recommendations to the man, the President, they'd been working with intimately, through a system that was manned, operated, and run by people who had been in the quote "illegitimate White House," the one White House that had been rejected, the one that had resigned. And so there seemed to be a division in the place when I arrived. I came in and was dumbfounded by it and can remember visiting with the President and telling him I didn't think I was the guy to do that job for a couple of reasons. One was the environment being what it was. And second, that I wasn't comfortable with the spokes of the wheel idea. I had trouble believing that we would be able to sufficiently order the affairs, complex affairs of government, if he had all these different pieces reporting directly into him. And that was when he kind of focused on that issue of order vs. disorder, in my mind, spokes of the wheels vs. some more orderly pyramid arrangement. And he kind of, mentally, made some qualifications in his earlier preference and recognized need for more order and at that point started moving towards it. I don't know if that answers your question.

GOLDWIN: Well, it begins to, Don. I think of some other things: the way the President's time was scheduled before you took over; the flow of paper in and out; decisions made that no one else or not enough people knew about; the preparation of speeches (the procedures that were used); and the decision procedures, the greatest example being the Nixon pardon. All of those things were connected not only as institutional problems but also as personality problems. Personality clashes were an aspect of institutional procedures, and if you omit those things you omit a very important part of the description of the Ford White House. I have in mind Robert Hartmann especially, but also other very senior people.

STORING: Another side of what you have suggested is that the White House organization isn't or wasn't simply an extension of Ford's disposition and intentions and inclinations, because as a matter of fact according to your account his inclination was in one direction but in fact, I take it under the press of the real world and with some advice from various people he really made a fairly significant shift.

RUMSFELD: Well, he was also getting that same advice from most elements in the White House. In other words, if you take Bob Hartmann, whose name has come up, Bob felt very strongly that something should happen differently than was happening and, I am told, was supportive of my coming in. And my impression was that most people had a concern that what was happening wasn't serving the President, or the country, well. And they liked that man, and they respected that man, and they wanted things to go well for him, and they wanted to be a part of something that was going well.

*   *   *

STEIN: Well, I think there's another option or maybe a suboption to Don's two ways of organizing things: one in which everybody has access and feels he's a participant; and the other is the President is closeted with a variety of papers submitted to him. And that is that there is a possibility of delegating the role of giving everybody access. And I think that has worked well at times in the period that I remembered when George Shultz was in charge of everything having to do with the economy. I think he was a master of getting everybody, cabinet members, the White House people, executive office people, and so on to feel that they are participating and to either come to agreement or come to agreements about the options and the issues in a way which relieved the President of a tremendous burden but didn't leave everybody else mad. But that's also very much a matter of personality. The same power delegated to somebody else operated in an entirely opposite way. But I think that there are possibilities of organizing—well, many people have the idea that (inaudible) sub-Presidents or assistants who can operate in bit fields and do a lot of the things that we expect the President to do. I think *there* was a case where for a couple of years it worked pretty well.

KEELEY: It would seem to me that the contrast between this loose and more ordered system of making decisions would have a very strong influence in the interaction between the staff members in the White House among themselves and the executive branches of the government. And I wonder if you would comment on that, whether in fact it does have some difference in the way you interact among each other and whether this is a bonus effect perhaps in the loose system.

RUMSFELD: It seems to me one of the parts of the answer may be that people do tend to have some bias for that which they've been doing. And what you had in this case of Mr. Ford coming in was a situation where half to three-quarters of the people, four-fifths of the people, had been doing it a certain way and we were used to it that way. And a new President comes in. He has a different way of doing it, somewhat. Everything we are talking about here is, as Herb (Stein) suggests, really a mix, a matter of degree. There aren't clean pigeon-holes for these different approaches. But it is much harder for someone who had developed a mode of working with Mr. Nixon to have that mode changed, much harder than for a new person coming in.

LYNN: To the extent it's a spokes of the wheel approach where somebody has on a regular or irregular basis the opportunity to come in and see the President with a more or less open agenda and discuss what's on his mind, you can sap away a tremendous amount of energy of the other players, because the other players, as they get to know the personality of their counterparts, their peer group, are scared to death about what's going on in that one hour meeting. And this is true no matter what the role is. And you wonder what kind of nefarious thing out of left field they're going to get into a casual discussion on, and whether a President is going to succumb to even giving the slightest signal to that person that he agrees. Because it is a truism in government that when you walk in as a pleader you will look, not in a Machiavellian way—because that's just the way we are as human beings—for any sign that the President agrees, and then some people will build on that and come out and say, "Well, the President's decided so and so." And this can range all the way from saying it's something like he's going to meet on to saying he's decided it substantively.

Now when those things happened the people that are department heads and agency heads feel that they're going to be measured by how many times they're going to get in to see the boss. You are measured on frequency of visitation, and we saw a fair amount of that in the Nixon years. And that wasn't limited to the Nixon years, don't get me wrong; it was true in prior administrations, too, and perhaps a little bit in the Ford administration. But I think far less because there were all these opportunities in the more structured method of the papers, the paper presentations, the task force discussions where the cabinet officers were brought in, and other agency heads, around a set of issues, who has a legitimate concern in this area. And to the extent that the President kept to his own system, I think he was pretty darn good at it. And one of the reasons would be that you, Rummy (Rumsfeld), would tend to be in there, at many of those so-called one-on-one meetings, or

Dick (Cheney) would be later and say, "Gee, that sounds interesting, Mr. President, but I would suggest what we do is put that into the system, and, George, will you spearhead getting a paper prepared on that?" And George, or Harry or Jane, or whoever it might be would feel at a loss at that point because "Ye gods who wants to see him use my view on his subject?"

So what I'm saying to you is I think that the spokes of the wheel approach with the access and the looseness of that arrangement is a disturbing and time wasting thing from the standpoint of *both* the people out in the departments and other people that are around the White House. There is more need, for example, if it's unstructured to have an office on the first or second floor of the White House rather than being over in EOB. If it's structured, you don't care about being in EOB and it was a hell of an advantage because you're with your own troops, if you're in OMB. And after all they're the people who are developing your positions and so on. You can spend more time with them. By the way if a secretary were really clever on this one-to-one thing, you come in on one thing on the agenda that's very innocent, something that Cheney or Rumsfeld is not going to be disturbed about and maybe the President isn't, but if you're clever what you do is you turn to get out of your chair and go to the door and say, "Oh, by the way, Mr. President," and hope very much that he'll react with something that is ambiguous enough that you can call it presidential decision.

CONNOR: That was the purpose of the system even before the President started to move that way. That is, if you came out with an unstaffed decision you still had to wave the decision around trying to figure out how do you make it happen. And the system was not sympathetic if it didn't come through us ...

LYNN: Or even when the decision *was* ...

RUMSFELD: As Herb said the kinds of things that probably come to a President and probably ought to come to a President tend to be things that are significant and that don't lend themselves to ready delegation to a single statutory officer. Take a grain embargo, take any export issue. Any export issue is at the same time a matter for the Agriculture Department, the Labor Department, congressional relations, foreign policy, maybe DOD—and all of those people have a legitimate statutory and a public responsibility. Or you take a decision like the Cost of Living Council would get into.

Like milk prices. No, that's a bad one. (Laughter) But those problems, simply don't lend themselves to pigeonholing with one statutory officer. And to make a judgment on, say, an embargo of sales to Poland, to make that kind of a decision in consultation with the secretary of agriculture alone is risky. To make that kind of decision with the secretary of state alone is risky—for the President, for the country, for the political party.

STORING: That's one question. Although another question is, granting that, how do you get the broader consultation that you want. I mean, one of the things that struck me when Jim Lynn was talking was that the pre-revisionist view of the presidency would regard the situation you describe as wasteful, and unnecessarily time-consuming, and inefficient, and so forth, as precisely the best way for the President to keep in charge. I'm only saying though that what you did, I'm simply stating as an interesting point that you gave a good account of the sort of Neustadt kind of view of the presidency which Neustadt thinks is *precisely* the way—just by keeping these subordinates off balance, by making them worry by what's happening, and so forth. That's exactly the way the President gets power and can use it.

LYNN: But Herb (Storing), what I am saying is that that goes on anyway. And therefore all you get out of a given system is bias. By that I mean you get a regular way of doing things. There would be, if you listen very carefully to what Rummy (Rumsfeld) said—is that on most kinds of issues we would go this way. And that's true because of the leak problem that he talked about, for example. That's why Abba Eban said in a speech in Cleveland many years ago that he believed in open covenants privately arrived at. There can be issues of that kind. There is an opportunity for that kind of a thing on a private basis once the matter has been staffed out. It was still a typical technique during the Ford years—with people particularly that were in close and had his confidence—that after the formal meeting on the way out, someone would follow him into his office and get a few other licks on something they didn't want to say in public because they didn't want it to appear in a newspaper, especially with staff. I was intrigued by Hess's comment that maybe you ought to take out the chairs along the rear. Well, I disagree with taking the chairs out. You can impose discipline in a different way as to who's brought in and who isn't. But we should never give an impression that these things are one or the other. The question is the *emphasis* within the system.

Now the one other thing I was going to say is, what distorts all of these systems, in my judgment, is that for a variety of reasons—some good and some, in my judgment, although very human, there isn't a whole lot of justification for them in trying to run a system of government—a person does not fit the system in the sense that the President doesn't feel comfortable with that person's advice and yet the President will not make the changes in the people as you go along that are necessary to make either system work. And the reason Presidents are reluctant to do that is because the minute that person is fired he can play it one of two ways. He can be very quiet; or what he tends to do is to say, "He didn't know what he was doing, or he was blindsided by other people in the administration, and I am a hero, and I am now going to be a martyr now that I've left." And what President needs that, presswise? And there are a number of other reasons for it. But what happens is once a team is put together there is not the flexibility in the changing of that team as time goes by. And one of the things I would think people studying the insitution should think of is, a) what are the ways, what are the conditions under which change ought to be made, and b) how can that be made easier. And I don't know how it can be. The process of firing is as a human matter the most difficult thing anybody who cares about people ever goes through. And we see, Hess talks about moving people around, different chairs, creating roles for them and so on. And all those tools are used.

But that, to me, is the real key aspect. The key aspect is you never know in advance of appointing somebody how they're really going to work out. It's like what they say about marriage. You really don't know your spouse until you've been married to him or her a while. Sometimes you're lucky and sometimes you're not. Now how do you gracefully, in the best way, make it easier for a President to make those adjustments in a team as you move along?

RUMSFELD: Everything you've said is true, but *the* most important time is the earliest time. Every day, every hour that goes by you lose options: you lose flexibility, you nod when you should have shaken your head; you shake your head when you should have nodded; you hire a person who has a whole set of attributes and biases or preferences and he goes out and makes thousands of decisions. And that early period is absolutely critical.

STORING: And it's the time when the President probably knows the least about the job and when he has to make quantitatively many more of those crucial decisions. Hess suggests that presidencies really depend on metabolism, and I'm about a two-hour man. (Laughter) So I would suggest that we take a short five minute break, and stretch, and then come back with another hour before lunch.

SECOND SESSION

Discussion here of alternative ways of organizing the White House staff and changes in the Ford White House staff system.

*   *   *

CONNOR: When we talk about good decisions in a presidential perspective I don't think we need to talk about substance of the decision: is this wise economic policy or not? The purpose of a system is to say that a good presidential decision is one in which the President is not surprised at what happened after that decision was made, that he has been informed, that he is going to get this kind of flak or that kind of resistance. For our discussion purposes, when we talk about a good decision, the system is designed to keep him from being surprised. He's the one who makes the choice. And he may get enormous resistance; it may be unpopular, or whatever. I think we have to keep that notion in mind. If the system worked, it worked not in the sense that he made a politically masterful decision or that he made one with marvelous consequences; but when he made it he knew what was likely to happen in many different areas, most of which were not immediately obvious prior to the decision. He didn't . . .

RUMSFELD: A staffing system should get things to the President in an orderly way so he knows what's going to happen, and makes a judgment. But he's perfectly capable of making a wrong judgment.

STEIN: Well, the system that's being described here by many of its practitioners as being substantively neutral and with respect to outcomes—that it's just a way of making sure that the President knows everything he is supposed to know—what people worry about the system is whether the custodians of the system are using their position astride the channels of communications to influence the outcome in a way that they are not legitimately expected to do.

CONNOR: Herb, that is a valid concern.

LYNN: But I will say to you, Herb, the monumental step forward in this process, in my judgment, is that if the people in the White House or in OMB know—when they've done the consultative job, and they've gotten the views of the various shops, and they're trying to put the distillate of that, the pros and cons, options, facts, and everything else, in the paper—that that paper is going to be reviewed, or can be reviewed, by the cabinet heads, it creates a discipline against tilting the paper that is very very good.

STEIN: Well, this back and forth is not endless. There is the final answer. Somebody has the last word. And, of course, there's—I guess I think of the OMB a little differently from the others because I think of OMB as ...

LYNN: Evil. (Laughter)

STEIN: No, I think of them as having a legitimate substantive role. They *are* the watchdogs of the money, and they are the people who are charged with assessing costs and benefits and so on. I wouldn't consider them to be a part of the problem. Well, I never knew what to think of John Ehrlichman, whether he was a substantive decision-maker or whether he was part of the process of getting papers in and out. And, well, it's a confusion.

CHENEY: But aren't you always going to have the problem, and it's merely a matter of degree depending on who's actually manning the system. Those people—which includes almost everybody in the administration who deals with the President through that process—are going to ask themselves the question of whether or not the process has integrity. Most of the time he's not going to get one hundred percent response. That is to say, the chairman of CEA, or the secretary of treasury, or the secretary of HUD, the head of OMB, is going to put something through that system and it's going to come back modified. He's going to get half a loaf because of the considerations which will have been added to his views, and the President will make a decision that takes them all into account.

The danger of not having a system seems to me is that it's not a matter of the cabinet secretary maliciously not having a presidential perspective—he's got the perspective of the cabinet secretary. The secretary of state gets paid to worry about our international political relationships, not our domestic political considerations. And unless you've got a system, you end up with all your specialists who are part of the process, that the only guy who's got an overview, is aware of what's going on in every area, is the President. And he's the only one who can make the decision. But if you follow the spokes of the wheel model instead of the pyramid model, I would argue, and have before, that everybody in the White House with very few exceptions is a specialist, not a generalist. And that if you took and asked the people who served President Ford in those senior spots how much of his (Ford's) time is devoted to their substantive policy area, economic or national security or whatever it was, and added up those percentages, you'd get three or four hundred percent. None of them know everything else he's doing except for those people who man that system, who see all the paper and see all the people and have a sensitivity and an awareness to his view of the world. And it's not a matter of using the process to get a specific policy outcome that the manager of the process wants to have. It's a matter of knowing that when something comes in from the international side that there is something else going on in the domestic area, and that the two need to be meshed.

STEIN: Well, that's the ideal description of the system. What I'm trying to get at is whether that is the real description of the system.

CHENEY: That depends on the people in the system.

STEIN: Sure, there is a very great demand on the self-restraint and responsibility of the people who are playing the role . . .

CONNOR: That's exactly where you come out. In the final analysis the presidency depends on character and personality as well as institution. In the end you can either corrupt any institution or you can create an institution that can prevent bad things from happening by preventing anything from happening. That's your dilemma. In the end it is the people who make the system work, whether it be the President or the people who work for him, it is their character you are talking about. Do they want to corrupt the system or don't they?

RUMSFELD: But there's a correcting mechanism, Herb (Stein). To the extent an individual standing astride that system lacks the integrity or views his job differently from one that would see that the President gets that information and can make the judgment as opposed to biasing the system himself, it gets around pretty fast. Then there's a much greater premium for people to circumvent the system, and then he is no longer sitting astride the system. On the other hand, ninety-nine percent of the time I didn't offer an opinion. But I mean if you take something like this energy independence agency that was proposed, I finally walked in and told the President I felt so strong about it that he just had to know, and I wanted to submit a separate memo on it. It looked like it was going to happen, and I've been sitting there kind of running it through in a nice objective way. Jim Connor was in on that—and it boggled my mind how strongly I felt against it. And so I just walked in and said, look, I'm going to come around the side and tell you how strongly I feel about it. But I did not bias the system.

STEIN: I think that's an open process.

RUMSFELD: But I didn't communicate my opposition to everyone else in the system.

STORING: There are two aspects of this question, going back partly to what Dick Cheney said. One is the question of fidelity on the part of the people who are running it; and the other is the question of whether the system itself somehow has certain consequences. I take it that the kind of argument that Hess represents is a concern that quite apart

from the fidelity of the people who are running it, or their devotion to the presidential view, and objectivity, and so forth, there is something about that system that is a hindrance. And one of the things that Dick Cheney said that tended to support that, it seemed to me, because you made the observation that most of that large and growing staff in the White House are in fact specialists, like the department people, and yet . . .
_____Is that bad?

STORING: Well, I don't know, except that presumably the purpose of the White House staff—presumably the overall purpose is to formulate and support a presidential view. If you have a huge and growing staff, the massive portion of which is a reflection of the same departmental or partial views that you have at the department level, you do wonder whether you've only brought your problems up and given them another level.

CHENEY: But I would argue, Herb (Storing), that to the extent you get specialists in the White House it is a reflection of the enormous complexity of the issues that the President has to deal with and the enormous malorganization, misorganization, whatever you want to call it, in the federal government. In other words, Brent Scowcroft isn't there as a representative of the Defense Department, or the State Department, or the CIA. He's there because there are a whole set of issues that involve all of those people, and the director of the CIA doesn't have the perspective of the secretary of defense. And somebody's got to pull those together and make sure all those views are represented and then go to the President.

. . . (inaudible) . . .

LYNN: He's a specialist in your perfect world and Steve Hess's perfect world in part. The perfect world is that each cabinet officer who has all the qualities you would want to have and that cabinet officer takes the final look at the paper before it goes across the President's desk, notwithstanding the time pressures on that cabinet officer to give speeches, to interview with the press, to testify and everything else. That person, when he has something in housing, or energy, or whatever it is, goes about calling his fellow cabinet officers together, and they hammer it out, and they come up with an agreement as to what should come in the paper. And that cabinet officer is going to be able to draw it all together and put a paper together. In other words, whichever one had the lead, that Henry Kissinger's going to call, or Don Rumsfeld is going to call, Earl Butz and say, "Now look, fellows, we've got to get together and we've got to get a paper for the President."

Now, I'd like to work toward that kind of cabinet officer—who is "straight up" no matter what kind of special interest group pressure he's got and ignores the fact that he's measured by the public on how much more money he's spending. You are a favorite with the interest group if you got more money, period. That's all that counts. Not that the programs worked better; you got more money and you got more programs. You're innovative, bold, ambitious. That means new ideas, new spending. Let's face it, that's been so since the Depression. Since the Depression at least, that's been the attitude. Program-a-minute club.

Now, I think everyone will agree you don't want to have forty papers going into the President. He hasn't got time to read them. In other words, the alternative thing you could do here to get cabinet input is to have each cabinet officer write his own paper; don't insist on them getting together on the papers; and have that pile of papers, twenty of them, come into the President; and ask the President of the United States to plow through twenty papers all in different lengths, none addressing the same issue on the same page, not meshing on the arguments, whether policy considerations or political considerations.

RUMSFELD: Not eliminating fact uncertainties.

LYNN: That's right, not even stating the facts. So now you come to the point, gee, wouldn't it be nice if you had one paper for the President. Now, where that process can get wrecked and ruin a President can be that whoever is preparing that paper truly is at the top of a pyramid. And I get worried about this pyramid vs. spokes of the wheel, because we didn't have a pyramid system in the Ford White House by way of the substantive input. The only pyramid we're talking about is in the area of, to some extent, access to the President, to a very limited extent, and that doesn't include cabinet officers. But every interest group in the world wants to see him, and there's got to be some kind of control valve that helps the President in that regard.

CHENEY: No, but lets . . .

LYNN: Now wait a minute . . .

CHENEY: . . . focus on the decisionmaking process.

LYNN: But on the decisionmaking process it wasn't a pyramid.

CHENEY: It was a pyramid in the sense that there was only one spoke through which the paper was to go.

LYNN: But the preparation of the paper, the oral discussion, and everything else was fully participatory.

CHENEY: We have semantic problems.

RUMSFELD: Jim (Lynn), the distinction, though, is the one that the President addressed in the transition team. When I came in he addressed it, and it was that, while he would have multiple sources of information in and up and around, that there would be a single channel for decisionmaking and that would be the staff system.

. . . (inaudible) . . .

CAVANAUGH: I just think there's another distinction between the two presidencies. One is that Mr. Nixon apparently had two or three people on his staff that he had great confidence in, that he delegated a great amount of decisionmaking to. And although they maintained a pyramid system, and a staffing system, and a system that ensured that all points of views from cabinet members were reviewed, that from time to time certain staff members made decisions on behalf of the President without a lot of direct presidential involvement. That apparently was Mr. Nixon's desire and way of organizing his White House. I think, on the other hand, with Mr. Ford there was a great view in terms of not only spokes of the wheel and having access even though the decision process went through the staff secretary, but that he wanted to be more a part of the decisionmaking process and in fact wanted to make more decisions on key policy differences between members of the cabinet and between the staff.

LYNN: But even where he made the decision, you've got to refine that a little bit. What I found, in the Nixon years, was that he would make decisions. But the question was whose views were known when he made them. In other words, he did delegate a number of decisions in two different senses. One, he didn't even want to get involved in them, and the person would be able to say that this is the decision of the White House. But in other cases, the oral discussion, *he* made the decision but it was on the basis of having read the papers, which on the whole were well done—to the extent I ever got to see them—and then would have oral conversation with just the staff in close to him. Now, if you're out there in the boonies, the way you learn to work that system was, and if they basically trusted you—the people that *were* discussing it with President Nixon—then the trick was for you to find the right opportunities to get in close to that staff person who *was* going to talk to the President so that your views would be known. That's a very *ad hoc* way of getting your way if you're a cabinet officer. I think I was fairly effective at it, though.

CHENEY: Who's going to make the judgment about which system though is good and which one is bad? Ultimately it's got to be the President.

LYNN: That's right.

CAVANAUGH: Exactly.

CHENEY: And if he chooses not to talk to anybody to make a decision, that his prerogative. I'm reluctant to get into a situation where we—there's implicit criticism in talking about the way the Nixon system worked sometimes or the way you talk about not having seen the papers when they went in, or that he sat down and didn't consult with you, the cabinet members, but consulted with a small number of staff. I really think that's a decision that only he can make.

... (inaudible) ...

LYNN: I'm not saying anything is moral or amoral. I'm saying, what system for the country will best fit, and I'm saying that no matter how good, it does involve the personality of the person who is President and what that person is comfortable with. But there are enough things, it seems to me from my own experience of eight years in the government, where it serves the public interest for those views to be heard.

CAVANAUGH: But the institution of the presidency in terms of what we're talking about indicates that a President can develop his system, and if he's comfortable with that system, that's the system that's going to be in operation. Right?

LYNN: But I'm saying that if the consequences of the system are bad, then that's not a very good system. Or are you saying (inaudible) . . .

RUMSFELD: There tends to be a criticism of the system, when in fact the criticism probably ought to have gone to the decisions being made by the President if a person disagreed.

STORING: That's possible, although that in a way is exactly one of the issues. I mean whether that's true, or whether on the other hand there is this process of bureaucratization, or centralization, or whatever, that really had a kind of independent life.

RUMSFELD: I can take dozens of things that were highly criticized in the press or by cabinet officers in both administrations as the fact that people tend not to want to criticize the President. And they blame it on Ehrlichman, or they blame it on the staff in the White House, or they blame it on the system or the procedures used, or they blame it on OMB, when in point of the fact it was working exactly the way the President wanted it to, doing exactly what he wanted, and he may be very happy to have that buffer out serving as a lightning rod for him.

STORING: I think this should be linked up to something maybe we could talk a little more about after lunch, which is the question of implementation. As a matter of fact, I'm not a Hess advocate, but one of Hess's points, of course, is that—most of you people talk in terms of decisionmaking, by which you've meant deciding what the policy is going to be, generating the ideas, and all the rest of that. And as a couple of people indicated earlier, a weakness seems to have been at the level of implementation. One of Hess's points is that this process of building this big system of decisionmaking at the policy level has, he claims, resulted in a kind of ossification which has led, on the one hand, to the White House taking responsibility for implementation but without the capacity for it.

CONNOR: Two points, one to follow up on Don (Rumsfeld). It is not only in our system. In the old imperial Russian system the Czar was good, but he had bad advisors around him. In every political system, the people want to believe in their leaders. They have to believe in their leader. So instead of wrestling with the hard questions of character we talk about systems, we like to seek comfort in systems and mechanisms that can be changed to protect us. And nobody in this country or elsewhere wants to come down and confront the question mentioned, and somebody was going to mention it sooner or later, the huge and growing White House staff.

STORING: I don't think I said, "huge." I said "large."

CONNOR: I want to take this opportunity to . . .

BESSETTE: We have a record.

RUMSFELD: This can be released to the public. (Laughter)

CONNOR: Steve Hess, Tom Cronin, and several other people with less qualifications have developed marvelous theories about the imperial presidency on the basis of size of the White House staff and budgets. The only problem with their theories, is that if anybody ever took the trouble to look, and I did, you cannot build a case on the imperial presidency by either looking at numbers of people or budgets of the White House. The greatest case of all is: FDR ran the White House with forty-five people. That's total nonsense. He did not run the White House with forty-five people. He ran it with somewhere around two hundred people. Kennedy ran it with a top number of 476; Johnson, 497, but probably about half again that much.

Nixon had one peak at 620, but generally was in the high 500s. Ford got it under 500; he actually did cut it. But if we are making arguments about an imperial presidency, and those arguments are based on either size of the White House budget or numbers of people on the White House staff, you'd better forget it. You cannot document that proposition. And every one of these arguments starts with the assertion that a small group of people once was the non-imperial presidency—not in modern memory.

CAVANAUGH: Which makes the case again, it's not the system, or in this case the size of the staff, or the budget. But in large part it's the man who sits in the Oval Office.

CONNOR: That really is the point I want to make. You can argue that there is an imperial presidency, you can argue greater roles of the President in the system, but you have to argue that from external factors: how the media treats Presidents, how that's changed over time, what is expected of Presidents, what is the nation looking to him for. Those are the kinds of questions that are worth discussing if you are discussing an imperial presidency vs. some other role. But theories which depend on numbers of people and how they're organized around the President I think are, first of all, factually wrong, and I think even in terms of how human nature works they are likely to be wrong.

STORING: Nobody to my knowledge has ever done a good fair accounting of that, that took into effect the detailees and other things of that sort.

CONNOR: Well, anybody here that wants it I will give them one, every year from 1934 on.

STORING: Very good, I'll bear that in mind.

CEASER: There's a certain number of points. One thing, in preparing I read not only Hess but (Francis) Bacon, and he made this comment on counsel. He said, "It's of singular use to princes (I supposed you could say Presidents) if they take the opinions of their council separately and together. For private opinion is more free and opinion before others is more reverent." And I think the "individual" element represents the spokes of the wheel; "before others" represents the pyramid. And even if you would agree on your system that there is not an element attempting to prevent the opinions from coming to the

President, still I think you could say that the quality of the advice that reaches the President is going to be different. The staff may have a different view of risk than the President. They may want to take a good deal more time in seeing that these proposals are ones that he should hear. And there is a question also of what is encouraged by way of initiatives from people when they offer ideas. I can't believe—this following Hess—that the type of presidency that Johnson or Roosevelt might have had with the sort of slap-dash ideas coming out, I can't believe that that would come out of a pyramid system.

_____We had plenty of slap-dash ideas. (Laughter)

LYNN: Are you arguing whether that's good or bad?

CEASER: It may well depend on what's required at the time and what the President wants, but I think there is some correlation between organization and output of ideas even if you assume the men in the system of the pyramid are trying to be fair. Then I had a couple of other comments, one about coordination in the cabinet. The idea was expressed that the function of the staff is to coordinate because the cabinet always represents special interests, and therefore you have to have someone having presidential views. And I wonder that if to some extent that's not perpetrated by the system in which the staff assumes that function and the cabinet is relegated to the outskirts and (inaudible) . . .

LYNN: You misconstrued what I was saying. In an ideal system your cabinet officers would have a presidential perspective. This is one of the reasons why I think Steve (Hess) has opened the debate to a very important issue—the qualities of the cabinet officers and what you're really looking for in the cabinet officer. The qualities of the cabinet officers ought to drive the system of organization in the White House to a very large degree. But what I am saying to you is at least based on historic fact. The historic fact is that most people appointed to cabinet officers after a period of time for one reason or another go inward toward their own missions under the battering that they take constantly by interest groups. And even if they try to be objective they are no longer capable of it. And it is the hardest thing you fight day after day when you sit out there in the department headquarters. To be negative, and you are always negative, if you don't want to spend the last buck they, the special interest groups, want to spend. The most impossible job in the world, probably, is to be the consumer assistant to the President. The only way you could win with a consumer group is to do the thing that the way-out-on-the-rim, most flakey consumer advocate wants. Because that's the only press that will be there.

CEASER: Well, I can make another point, that the Ash Commission addressed this point and said maybe the problem is in the structure of the cabinet.

LYNN: What did he mean by that?

CEASER: Well, he suggested that it's because the cabinet is spread out and organized along interest group lines without having the coordination built into the cabinet so that the cabinet officer would be forced to do the coordinating.

LYNN: There is no way; that is one of the greatest fallacies to mankind. And if I were to criticize one of the things the new administration is doing it is this fantastic overblown priority given to reorganization. I think there is room for reorganization, and it can be useful. But there's no way on the very things that Don (Rumsfeld) was talking about in today's world and get even close to ever putting in any one department or agency, no matter how well you reorganize them, all of the competing missions, goals, and priorities that will bear on the major problems of this country. Whether they are energy, whether they are economic issues, whether they're national security, whether they're housing programs, welfare programs—tell me any organization structure that will not require coordinated task force approaches cutting across the departments. There is no . . .

CEASER: The Defense Department was originally different departments, and I think that the institution of . . .

LYNN: It can be improved, but to think it will ever get rid of the need for coordination is just absolutely false.

CHENEY: If you had absolute total authority to organize it any way you want it tomorrow, you could not come up with a structure that's going to solve the problem of the need of a President for staff to help him sort through . . .

RUMSFELD: One thing you could do is to take the people who have served in the departments and have them serve some time in OMB and in the White House, and have the people who have worked in the White House serve some time in the departments and agencies, at least for a period of time.

GOLDWIN: I think Jim (Lynn) is right that the problem is so fundamental that you can rearrange things but you can't get rid of it.

CONNOR: You shouldn't ever be able to get rid of it. You're talking about issues like energy . . .

LYNN: Competing goals and objectives, always.

CONNOR: But the real question is not putting a number of boxes that have energy in their title in the same department. The critical energy issues in this country are tradeoffs between energy demands and environment, national security, and the economy. And you're not going to have all those three things coordinated under energy. Do you even want to?

. . . (inaudible) . . .

GOLDWIN: Take one example that was a problem early in the Ford administration and persists: the food reserves, food assistance, and food sales. However the government is organized, that subject is going to have problems that are dealt with by Treasury, State Department, Agriculture, Commerce, and OMB. However you're organized, there's going to be a budget problem, a foreign policy-diplomacy-alliance problem, a balance of payments problem, and so on. You couldn't imagine some *one* agency that would take care of all those things, because if it did then it would have to have subordinate agencies that would immediately begin to reflect the same responsibilities and therefore biases.

_____ But then the cabinet minister would be the mediator.

... (inaudible) ...

GOLDWIN: It gets back to the point that Dick Cheney was making about generalists and specialists. There must be someone who feels that it is his responsibility to take care of the balance of payments problem and to worry about whether we're going to get any revenue from shipping our food abroad. There must be someone who feels responsible for that, who feels the pressure for it, and who will make the case as persuasively as possible to the President when a decision has to be made about food sales or food assistance. So that it's inevitable that there will be specialists. Otherwise the government isn't going to work and people aren't going to feel reponsible for things that are of very great importance. But since the President has to take into account in a general way all of these elements, he'll be alone in thinking of it that way if he discusses it only with cabinet members. So he wants to have around him a few people who have the responsibility to see these problems from *his* viewpoint. Therefore, I think it's inevitable, however you organize, that there will be a White House staff with some kind of second guessing of the highest constitutional officers, the cabinet members, and there will be that kind of resentment. Cabinet members don't act presidential and say, "I know this would be very good for our diplomatic relations with a nation, but I understand OMB's concern about the cost of giving this food away, so let's not do it."

LYNN: No, occasionally it happens.

GOLDWIN: But he's got responsibilities to his department.

... (inaudible) ...

STORING: Gentlemen, I'm sorry we have a logistics requirement if you want time for a drink before lunch, we have to stop now, and I trust that you do.

THIRD SESSION

STORING: I have a couple of things that I'd like to do. Let me mention two first. I do want to be sure that everybody gets an opportunity or takes an opportunity before we close to at least state questions that you might think we should or should have talked about that we haven't talked about. In other words, I would like to lay it down as a rule that nobody may leave and then after he leaves say, "What we should have talked about there was so and so," without at least having said that at some time, so that we have that on the agenda. I won't guarantee that we will in fact have talked about all those questions, but I really want any judgments you may have of that kind. But I think before coming to that I would like to—I originally opened the discussion with a question that invited the response of the people from the Ford White House and may have somewhat discouraged some of the others from jumping in as quickly as they might otherwise have done. So I would like to open the floor with special invitation to the people here from the University of Virginia to see if they have comments, or reactions, or questions that we ought to be discussing that we haven't. So let me do that.

HENRY: Well, o.k., let me push the Steve Hess argument and perhaps see how far that goes. Accepting what Jim Lynn was saying about the likelihood that department heads are not always going to think presidential, and accepting that, no matter how we push the pieces around, the federal government is not going to be organized so that everything is in nice neat places, Hess is pushing two arguments. First, granting that you've got to have the staff process to bring these things together, how do you keep that mill from grinding fire and fire and fire? Now, as I understand what he is saying, Hess says one way you do it is by ruthlessly, almost arbitrarily, limiting the number of people in the White House so that of necessity they have to pick and choose, exercise the staff coordination only on the most central and crucial issues. I think he's saying, secondly, that to the extent that you build these staff processes you make them more acceptable and legitimate if you append them more directly from the department heads or the cabinet itself as a collectivity rather than having them depend from the President himself in a personal fashion. I'm not arguing for that position, but I'd like some reaction to that to test the outer limits of the Hess argument.

CONNOR: Let's start with the proposal to "ruthlessly limit the number." I mentioned earlier most discussions of the White House staff proceed on a total ignorance of what the numbers really were and they compound that with a complete lack of understanding of what those people do who are, in fact, in the White House. You've got 485 people in the Ford White House, with maybe twenty-five detailees. Fully half of those people are engaged, more than half, three-quarters of those people are engaged is essentially clerical functions, as the secretaries to the staff officials and that whole group called the operating offices. They do not have formal career protection but they have *de facto* career protection. So the real numbers are down even from that four or five hundred number well into the range of below one hundred people. In that number you have people who are engaged in certain kinds of activities that I think everyone would agree really ought to be appropriately done in the White House. One is liaison with the Congress. You have some number of people who are going to be doing that. If you count up how many people you need to deal with 535 people, all of whom think they are important, you've got to have somebody to answer their calls and answer their letters and hold their hands. It turns out you have to have about fifteen or so people to do that.

RUMSFELD: All of whom *are* important. (Laughter)

CONNOR: I think I'll stick with my description.

LYNN: They *are* important.

CONNOR: Well, some of them may not even know what they are voting on.

GOLDWIN: Jim (Connor), in those numbers, are you including the Domestic Council staff?

CONNOR: No.

GOLDWIN: OMB?

CONNOR: No.

GOLDWIN: Council of Economic Advisors?

CONNOR: No.

LYNN: But OMB isn't any bigger than it was.

CONNOR: OMB has not grown at all in years. In fact, it's smaller than it was in 1946. There's a press office. Some substantial number of whom are engaged in the care and feeding of the press. Now, that doesn't have anything to do with policy coordination, cabinet officers making decisions, and the like. It's making sure that the reporters don't get lost.

STORING: That's not quite true, that it's not pertinent to this broader thesis, because if I remember one of the arguments is precisely that the press office tends to centralize the information function in the government as a whole. It is either an instrument of that or the cause of it. So it's connected to this broader question.

. . . (inaudible) . . .

STORING: Maybe not, but it's a fact, it's a phenomenon. It may not be bad, but the argument at least is that the control and release of information in the U.S. government tends more and more to be channeled through the White House. And that may be right or it may be wrong, but it's argued anyway that that's a change.

GOLDWIN: Herb (Storing), simple facts show that that's wrong. Take the press office of the Defense Department or HEW. They're twenty or thirty times bigger than the press office of the White House.

CHENEY: The PR shop at Defense has more people than the whole White House staff.

GOLDWIN: This notion of centralizing doesn't come from the staff size.

STORING: Then the question would not be in terms of numbers. I mean, what kind of policies—you may well be quite right, but is it true that major policies that might at one time have been announced by a cabinet officer or his press people now tend to get announced by the White House? Now I mean that may simply not be true.

RUMSFELD: Compared to what? The answer is, yes, compared to the Johnson administration.

CONNOR: Compared to the Eisenhower, Kennedy, Truman and Roosevelt administrations—no.

SCOWCROFT: But I think that the real fact is that it's not dependent on the size. It's dependent on the President's judgment as to where it's most effective to have it announced. Size is irrelevant.

CONNOR: It is also dependent on another phenomenon which has nothing to do—and on this I want to be very careful—with the Hess structural, numerical arguments. It is a function of the way in which media can focus on a President, and ask questions, and get answers. Things which would not play if they came out of the department or agency will play if they come out of the White House. So that although certain of those phenomenom may be taking place, there is more attention to the presidency. It is not a function of structure or numbers. And when you make these grandiose arguments about it, you've missed the damn point.

LYNN: I'll give you the practical side. The major newspapers have reporters that cover the White House and other reporters who cover departments and agencies. I think there's a healthy competitive instinct between the two on who gets the story. And I recall that in the Ford administration we made a conscious effort more and more to—when questions were asked at a White House press briefly about something that was happening in a department, to have the press officer say, "Go to the department and find out about it, or *we'll* go to the department and get an answer from the department." And it would be published as a departmental answer. The White House press corps did not like that one bit, because they didn't want the story coming from the Defense Department reporter; the White House reporter wanted it to come from the White House reporter. So having once been in this over a period of many years, even when you have the right bias to move it out into the departments and agencies—and I recall discussions on this, Dick (Cheney)—it was very very hard to implement because the White House press corps didn't want it implemented. So I'm just giving you the practical side of it.

RUMSFELD: Since you said you didn't want people to leave and then say they should have said something—the problem I have with the Hess discussion around the table is that it seems to me that it's an inappropriate vehicle to set the parameters of any discussion on this subject. We've been talking about effort and technique—I'm not talking about his analytical stuff in the beginning but the end of it where he's got these five new ways to solve the problems of the world. It seems to me that the times, the environment, the expectations that exist when one goes in, the press appetite is one, what has been, the personality of the President, as well as the approach or the technique or the effort are all important. And the effectiveness of what actually happens as a result is what's really important. If that's good or bad, it's perfectly appropriate to look back and say what were the things that contributed to that good or bad result. But to be led down a channel that suggests that organizational charts, or the things that he focuses on at the end of his book, are the answer as to why something turns out good or bad, if your measure is effectiveness I think it's chasing the wrong rabbit or at least it's looking at too little of the whole picture.

CHENEY: I think most of us who served in the Ford White House agree with that view.

RUMSFELD: Which makes it right. (Laughter)

STEIN: I think that we have ignored, that nothing has been said about a very dominant fact here, which is the change in the function of government, the expansion in the role of government, and the increased concern about interactions. That is, there was a time when the Department of Agriculture had an agricultural policy. It was not then a sub-branch of inflation policy, environment policy, energy policy, and so on. And if somebody had to look at all these interactions, it requires a central body and that central body is going to be much bigger than it used to be. When this fellow from the new transition staff talked to me about how to organize economic policymaking in the White House, I said, "Well, it depends. If you're going to have a Milton Friedman kind of policy, you need two or three people. If you're going to have a Leontiev kind of policy, you need four hundred people." I don't think there's any way to get around that. And we are moving more in the direction where we are concerned about what everything does to everything else.

STORING: And that's because we're doing more things.

STEIN: Well, yes, we're doing more things and we're taking more responsibility. So I think this is a case where form follows function, and that we are concerned about the inflation impact of everything, the environmental impact of everything, the energy impact of everything, the equal rights impact of everything, the women impact of everything. All of those interactions require geometrical multiplication. It's like one of Leontiev's tables: it increases by the square. And so I think that has a lot to do with the size of the staff.

STORING: I wanted to ask about another thing, the relatively small number of political appointees in connection with this question of controlling the bureaucracy. Is that an important consideration? Is that a point in the government at which it would make sense to think about changes? Would it make much difference in controlling the bureaucracy or guiding the bureaucracy if there were a significantly larger number than there is now of political appointees?

*　　　*　　　*

CHENEY: The number of political leaders in the administration, it seems to me, isn't nearly as important as the fact there is absolutely nothing you can do without an enormous investment in time and personal resources about reorganizing the bureaucracy and reducing it. There was a piece in the *(Washington) Post* recently that somebody had analyzed the Department of Agriculture and showed that out of 45,000 people in the course of a year, 44,996—all but four—got merit increases that year. A merit increase is for quality performance. They probably spent ten man years of effort to keep the four people from getting the merit increase. (Laughter) It's the inability to deal with the bureaucracy in a fashion that gives you anything that remotely resembles a personnel policy. You don't have a personnel policy. It just doesn't exist.

STORING: And it wouldn't significantly help if your political appointees were two or three levels down lower in the bureaucracy?

CHENEY: It would help, sure. But you've still got the problem of all those people underneath.

LYNN: What the Turkish government reportedly does is, in any given year the head of the agency has the right without restriction, other than doing it on political biases—in other words you can't do it because someone is a Republican or Democrat or Independent—to can one percent of the employees of the department without cause. For the purpose of the idea, it wouldn't make any difference whether it was one percent, one-half of one percent, a quarter of one percent. The idea is that those that really do know that they're substandard would all wonder whether they might be the one or ten or fifty that could get fired. So therefore it would give them some encouragement to at least raise themselves above that marginal level to get out of the danger zone.

STORING: By the way, you know, the original Civil Service law was perfectly rational in this respect, providing for no restriction on removal—the idea was you protect the appointment.

LYNN: This, like all things, is a very complex subject, because some of the very things that we are doing now in the name of ethics are things that, in my judgment, are destroying an incentive for talented, vigorous, bright, able, young people coming into the government that we had for years. Let me give you an example. The SEC overall has a quite competent staff and, as things go in a larger organization, so is IRS, and in their policy side, and so on. One of the reasons why you would attract bright young people to the SEC, the Anti-trust Division of the Justice Department, or to the FTC, or tax division, was they knew if they came into the government they had two tracks available to them. One, they might decide to stay—they liked it, and being involved in public policy and important issues was worth the sacrifice in pay that would be entailed. But another reason was, many of them looked upon it as the best degree, ticket, when they left to go out and make a heck of a good living. Now, today, it's put the other way—it's, quote, "revolving doors," unquote—and there is something very sinister about having gotten part of your training in an agency. We even see coming into laws things like in the Consumer Product Safety Act. That if you served there you can't have anything to do with the federal government in those areas for a minimum of two years after you leave. Now, I'm a great believer in our academic system, and I love professors dearly, but I would like to see people getting that training to have some sympathy for the problem of people in government when they come out into the private-for-profit sector. There's got to be balance brought to that. What I used to say in the speeches was sound: we have many people in the government we don't deserve. And I mean that at both ends. We have many people we don't deserve because they're not competent; and we have many people we don't deserve who are supercompetent, who have made real sacrifices by not going into the private sector. And there were many people of that kind.

One of the basic problems, I agree with Dick (Cheney), is that if you want to can somebody it takes an extraordinary investment in time to do it. The Civil Service Commission will be supportive. The courts will be supportive. But you've got to build a case like nobody's business before you actually go about the firing. But part of the problem in the federal government is that we have never worked out for ourselves a permanent management system. The people down the line in middle management are not measured by the job of management that they do. Very rarely has a President given a signal to his cabinet or to the agency heads that although day-to-day management is not my function as President, I want to pick people partially for their managerial ability with increasing parts of their time being spent on it as you move down into the shops. They're going to be measured on those management abilities; on how they turn on people with incentive, how they come up with systems so that you can recognize people that aren't performing, and so on. And I really think we tend to be too simplified about whether it's a career job or not. I saw an awful lot of schedule Cs who frankly didn't do a terribly good job. And many cases it wasn't because they weren't able, it wasn't because they didn't care, but because they weren't turned on by proper management techniques—that management was not given the kind of priority it should be. Now again, I think there were efforts made at that: for example, President Nixon's proposal, that we should have an executive management where, like a teacher, you have five years but at the end of the five years you come up for review; a technique where if someone really is bad that you could do something about it. What I'm saying is, I don't think it's as simple as career or noncareer.

But what you're getting at in the asking of these questions again is, in my humble judgment, the need for the staff, and Steve (Hess) says this, that the need for how many, quote, "specialists" you have, the need for people who have straight-up interests for the President to tell it to him straight, whether out of OMB or out of the Domestic Council staff, depends totally on the quality of the people that you are bringing in at the cabinet and departmental level, and what kind of a priority the President gives to various functions of those people, what he expects of them, and canning them, darn it, if they don't perform. And what we see here are a bunch of *ad hoc* arrangements, some of which will always be necessary. But the degree to which you have them will depend totally on what those qualities are of those cabinet and agency people and how much a President clearly gives signals to them on what their priorities ought to be and what he expects of them. And all the rest of it falls into place when you do that. But it also involves, as I say, that very delicate business of having to say every so often, Charlie or Jane or whatever it may be, you can't hack it. You're a lovely person and you're a great success in the private sector as a teacher, as an entrepreneur, as a foundation head, but this just isn't your thing.

That's why I said one thing we might all work on are better ways of gracefully moving someone out of a job, and that includes public acceptance principles, of getting it to a point where it can be done without making it impossible politically for the firer. To work in that area could be extremely useful.

SHANNON: Have there been studies made—and I'm not a political scientist—have there been studies made of the government bureaucracy here and comparable nations?

_____ Sure.

SHANNON: Can we learn anything from them?

LYNN: On this kind of a problem? Well, all I know is that when you sit down and eavesdrop on heads of state conversations, or if you are a cabinet officer and talk to your counterpart, whether it's in the Soviet Union or England, you'll find exactly the same thing in varying degrees.

*   *   *

CEASER: I just want to raise, I think, the obvious point. From the point of view of people in the administration the problem is how do we get control of the bureaucracy. But one should ask initially whether it's the prerogative of the administration to get full control over the bureaucracy.

LYNN: Define what you mean by control. I am very serious. If you define control as meaning attempting to see that people comport themselves in accordance with the politics and programs enunciated by the President of the United States, you darn well better get control.

BESSETTE: But what about the policies and programs in statutes?

LYNN: Now, wait a minute. I'm assuming that what the President of the United States has directed is consistent with the law of the land. And if you can prove that someone down the line is doing things that are inconsistent with the policies and programs, legal policies and programs of the President of the United States, you can can him. Because that is what the system is based on. Now, if you mean control over them in the sense that they are never going to utter a word in a meeting in trying to change some policy, nobody's for that.

CEASER: I'm speaking of interpretation of policies which are congressional laws and in which a bureau may have some discretion.

Is it his obligation to exercise that discretion in the spirit of the prevailing President, or in his own spirit, or in the spirit of what he took Congress to be?

CHENEY: For the most part in the executive branch, not speaking on regulatory agencies because they're a separate problem, I would argue very very strongly that he's got to carry out his authority to the best of his ability in line with what he thinks the President wants him to be.

STEIN: Well, the law doesn't usually delegate authority to a bureau head . . .

STORING: No, no, that's not . . .

LYNN: In writing a regulation you can interpret a statute five different ways.

CHENEY: If you don't have that fundamental linkage, that is, the concept the extent that an individual official in the executive branch is going to exercise his authority in accordance to the President's wishes, then you've totally broken down any sense of accountability at all. Nobody ever votes for that bureau chief or that GS-15 down in the depths of the organization. He is accountable to absolutely no one. The President is the only guy with his name on the ballot and everybody else in a hired guy. And once you begin to argue that that bureaucrat has the right to thwart presidential intent—you've destroyed the whole concept of how the democratic system operates.

CEASER: No, I think, I'm very sympathetic to this argument, but I'm quite aware that there are different arguments as to accountability and to the President's prerogative. I thought that this other view should be voiced because we're all beginning with the assumption which really comes out of the Brownlow Commission report, that the executive agent, the executive bureaucracy, is the President's. There have been different theories in American politics as to whether that's true and very different understandings of accountability, accountability to professional standards, accountability to Congress, and the like. I just raised this, I personally don't want to press it. There are instances where obviously we saw in the Nixon administration where accountability to professional standards might have offered a salutary check against the executive.

CHENEY: That wasn't a problem in the bureaucracy. That was a problem among the political appointees in the administration.

STORING: It is also a fact that an awful lot of statutory authority is vested not in the President but in the departments or agencies or secretaries. So that on that basis there is an argument—you see, I mentioned at the outset this Jackson vs. Whig view. You know the Whig view—against Jackson's notion which was sort of like the notion you've been putting, Dick (Cheney), which is that the administration was his hands and fingers, therefore, he had the right to fire the secretary of the treasury—the Whig view was the army is the army of the country, not of Jackson; the administration is the administration of the country not of Jackson. Now, again, neither do I want to simply press that argument, but there is a pretty respectable argument.

LYNN: A part of that is on the basis of convenience in the sense that everyone knows that if you say "the President of the United States shall," and they do that in many cases for a number of reasons—one is you want flexibility in a President to move around delegation of authority, but in most cases where it looks like a matter purely within a given department, what's the use of giving it to the President when you know the first thing you're going to have to do is create more paper, an executive order, that delegates it to the cabinet head. And being practical about it, if you look at the certificate you got as a cabinet officer, it says, "trusting in the integrity, judgment, and so on of the gentleman from Ohio," you are to serve at the pleasure of the President of the United States. And "for the time being"—those are the words. Congress knows when it passes a law that, sure, a secretary can do something contrary to what the President wants him to—but the reason for that "for the time being" is that if he gets too far off the reservation the President *is* the person that's accountable to the people ultimately through the elective process, and that secretary can go. So to try to draw a line on other than regulatory functions that require a kind of a law-like decision and say the President shouldn't get into the act really bothers me. Let me give you one of the best examples that I tried to get things generated on and never did.

STORING: Jim, just before you do, I just want to insert that that doctrine that you say bothers you is a modern doctrine. I mean it comes from the Myers case, and prior to the Myers case it was not by any means clear . . .

LYNN: Well, let me give you a very good example. We seem to have a theory in this country that when it comes to anti-trust policy and the bringing of anti-trust lawsuits on new theories, for example, that that should reside in the assistant attorney general in the Justice Department. And not only should the President of the United States not have a say about that, but, ye gods, the assistant attorney general shouldn't even consult the attorney general with regard to it. Now, I say to you that where those decisions involve macro-economic matters that can be of importance to the economy of the country, or could involve some overall policy with regard to deregulation, that it is a perfectly appropriate thing for the issue to be reviewed by the attorney general and on his judgment, or by memo from the President setting forth where he wants to be advised, to be reviewed by the President. It should be part of the established policy.

RHOADS: If it's on the record.

LYNN: Yes, if what's on the record, the fact that he consulted? Or do you want the *Wall Street Journal* sitting in the meeting? Just that they consulted him?

RHOADS: Well, what I was objecting to was the notion that . . .

LYNN: That it's covert?

RHOADS: Yes.

LYNN: Well, I'm saying to you the way I wanted to do it was by an executive order from the President making it clear that that's what was to happen, that this is my decision and you're going to follow it, and that this process shall be followed on as to process anything that will affect the economy or you may think we will have reason to believe will affect it in this way, or has a sensitivity in international affairs that will be of interest to other departments, etc. That things of that nature must come to the attention of the President of the United States.

LYNN: That's exactly what's reflected . . .

CHENEY: He's literally accountable to no one in terms of making those decisions. The American people can't hold him accountable for what he decides to do in a particular case. But somehow the morality of his position is automatically less suspect that that of the President, because the President is a politician and a political figure.

STORING: On the other hand, on the accountability point you mentioned a couple things; after all, in many of these cases there *is* another line of accountability, namely through the congressional committees. So it's not simply true that a bureau chief who resists presidential interpretation of the statute, it's not simply true that he's not accountable in any sense, because if he doesn't have some support in Congress it's likely to be hard, for just the reasons you described, for him to maintain . . .

Then that raises the question of what this sort of Brownlow Commission view of a hierarchical President—here's the President, here's the administration, and in an ideal world when the President says, "do it," then its' done—but where exactly does that leave the Congress in the system if you were to . . .

LYNN: Congress can get into any darn thing they please . . .

STORING: But you don't like that.

LYNN: That's my basic point, . . .

STORING: And that's legitimate?

LYNN: . . . and they do, but they get into the wrong things. That's the problem. (Laughter)

STEIN: If Congress wants something to be outside this hierarchy they can set up something like the Board of Governors of the Federal Reserve.

STORING: That also is a matter that would be in dispute constitutionally, how far the Constitution . . .

LYNN: When I made a controversial decision that supported a presidential policy I knew it wouldn't be more than two hours after it happened that hearings would be scheduled on it. So as far as the practical side of it is concerned, you knew you had oversight from two places: one above you, the President, and the other, the Hill. That's how it works in practical effect. And there's nothing wrong with that. I don't like sometimes the congressional sense of priorities—they'll often do it on the basis of what's news rather than on what's important. But to have it that way? Of course it ought to be that way.

*   *   *

SCOWCROFT: I think this could be one of the central areas that the Center might want to look into: the power of the presidency and its relationship to other . . .

STORING: You know, it's a very interesting point because of course the dominent academic view has been that the thrust in the direction of a stronger President is just invincible, and that although . . .

LYNN: It's changed so in the last . . .

STORING: Well, that is the question, whether the change is—and I'll say I'd be open on this one—whether the change is a wrinkle, or whether it represents, as has been suggested, a sort of more fundamental thing.

LYNN: I think it's a pendulum that is swinging the other way and it is continuing to swing even with the new administration. For example, one appropriation subcommittee resolution said, "Thou will not cut the '77 money for the water projects." He hadn't even proposed cutting the money. But this kind of relationship between the executive branch and the legislative, the signals back and forth, the irate calling of the witnesses as to who killed Cock Robin. Who was the person that advised the President on this? We want the paper that went into the President. This isn't any aberration; this is just a thing that's swinging back.
    Let me give you one of the best ones. There was a proposal that all new regulations by an agency shall lie before the committee in the

House or the Senate for at least sixty days before they become effective. Now, what follows from that is if Congress were going to carry out an oversight function, they damn well better have about the same kind of staff with the same expertise as the branch did. They ought to take all the time to read all of the hearings and all of the fact sheets, and they ought to have the benefit, should they not, of all the internal option memoranda that were used to prepare those regulations. That means getting into the day-by-day regulation. Now, I don't blame the Congress in many of these areas for wanting to do more, because on the one hand they've seen sometimes, what they consider, at least, an abuse of flexibility. On the other hand, they do not want to write the laws rigidly because they know that the work under the law has to evolve. So the compromise positions are one house vetoes, which is a way of having the half-way house, and the other way is the kind of other procedure that I just described. As things become more complex, they don't want to give up total flexibility to the executive. And on the other hand they realize they could put the whole country in a straight jacket if they write a law that has infinite detail.

BESSETTE: But on this point isn't it the case that it still remains fundamentally true that the executive branch has certain capacities and certain qualities and the legislative branch has certain capacities and other qualities. And the great capacity of the executive branch is for action. And presumably, or in principle, the capacity of the legislative branch is to deliberate and to reason about actions taken in other places. Isn't it the case that that really establishes the parameters in which this struggle occurs? And the example of that would be the energy policy that Carter recently came out with. It's clear that Congress didn't have the institutional capacity to develop a policy like that and probably not the political inclinations to take the heat. So doesn't that indicate that there are these various capacities, or qualities, of each branch which are related essentially to their constitutional nature, the one and the many, and that that really establishes the ground rules, or the parameters, in which this struggle will occur?

LYNN: I think I agree with some of that, but one thing you haven't mentioned is, there is no good reason under the Constitution why the

Congress could not be a bigger contributor and more powerful on overall broad policy formulation and programatic formulation. And . . .

BESSETTE: But there is, because there are 535 of them split in two.

LYNN: Now hear me out a minute. What has developed over the years in the executive branch are these coordinating mechanisms. And the coordinating mechanisms are things like the NSC; the task force; the budget reviews where people are brought together and competing viewpoints are brought in one room—the task force on drug abuse, on crime, on Vietnam refugees, whatever it may be. The Hill, due to its own structures, doesn't have that. Every standing committee looks at it with blinders on: "I don't want to hear what the competing priorities or missions are." Now the Budget Office was the first move toward trying to get a coordinated viewpoint. But the budget process, where you don't have one tie breaker as you do in the executive branch, therefore requires some overall coordinating mechanism to develop the policy and the programs that are brought into the budget process. That's why I said during the lunch break to somebody, one of the most exciting and important developments, in my judgment, on Capitol Hill in the last twenty-five years is Tip O'Neill's present efforts to form this umbrella committee on energy which will have the funneling job. We've talked about pyramids. This is an hourglass when they get the overall comprehensive proposals from Carter. They have the decision-making on what committees get what. They try to coordinate the actions of the standing committees. It comes back to the overall umbrella committee, but here's where I don't quite like what they're doing. The bill that goes to the floor will represent, if there's a difference between the standing committee and the umbrella com-mittee, the views of the standing committee. But the umbrella committee can put forth its own alternative proposal. I would have done it the other way around.

If Congress will come up with more of those kinds of umbrella coordinating mechanisms, one of the things you will find is there will be less need for a lot of the White House staff organizations that you have, and let me explain why. Because if those kinds of umbrella organizations on the Hill can be made to work, they will come up with what at least an executive believes is more rational policy. And they will, over a period of time. You'll crawl first and then walk in doing it. But one of the reasons why you have the inner-White House staff is that the cabinet officers have to deal with those heads of state in the standing committees who don't look at anybody else's jurisdiction. They get mad if a policy is put together by a cabinet officer dealing in liaison with some other cabinet officer because it doesn't jibe with the mission of their particular committee. The White House responds to the cabinet officer playing the game of the narrow jurisdiction of his department and the Hill by proposing a flakey proposal that isn't coordinated, and the White House has to respond with the only coordinating mechanism in town. So it isn't necessarily the nature of the beast that you have to have what . . .

BESSETTE: But there's one fundamental problem, namely that in Congress there isn't the same incentive for that individual congressman to vote in accordance with the umbrella committee's decision about the overall policy that there is in the executive branch.

LYNN: Oh, I agree with that.

BESSETTE: Because you still have some control down through a certain level.

STORING: Especially without party discipline.

BESSETTE: Without party discipline and without leadership.

SHANNON: I said the first time I spoke that I'm not a political scientist, I'm an historian. And the idea that the assertiveness of Congress is not likely to go away, I thoroughly agree, but I don't think it's anything new. It's been there a long long time.

Well, even when FDR was President. I don't think FDR understood organized labor, and it was Robert Wagner that got the NLRB through against the President's real wishes, but he wouldn't speak out against it. He didn't come out for it until is passed the Senate with nineteen dissenting votes. As for hemming the President in and getting legislation in that he didn't really want or getting (inaudible), look at the Neutrality Acts, 1935 and thereafter. Then you get back in the 19th century, remember the impeachment of Andrew Johnson. That was even more absurd. And I think it would be a mess if we didn't have an assertive Congress. It's a question of how they are assertive, what is the wisdom of their assertiveness.

CONNOR: I think it's a very useful point that Mr. Shannon made. It seems to me that in carrying out this discussion you've got to keep two very different things in mind. One is the historical viewpoint of the relations over time between executives and legislatures, it's not nearly as clear that things are one way or another. The second is what I call fashions of the presidency, the currently fashionable ideology, whatever that happens to be. And I think that in that line, to me at least, it is not clear which way that pendulum is swinging regardless of which way the congressional-presidential pendulum is swinging. If you will, Dick Neustadt's attitude, Arthur Schlesinger's attitude, MacGregor Burns' attitude, in retrospect they're not very different from attitudes about the Supreme Court in the '30s. They are attitudes that glorify institutions that are presumably generating the policy outputs that the particular writer of the article happens to think are very good. It is not suprising that you get very negative attitudes on the presidency appearing on the parts of the writers who are not congenial to Richard Nixon's policy, programs, approaches, beliefs, behavior. I think what's going to be interesting to see in the future is whether or not the fashion shift moves back again with a Carter in the White House. Or maybe Carter won't meet the needs, and maybe the fashion will continue. It seems to me there is a very big difference between the fashions of what people are saying is legitimate about a presidency—a presidency has got to be strong, a presidency has got to be weak—and the actuality of the continuing struggle between institutions, each of which are trying to take advantage of the other, probably as they were set out to do.

BAX: I have a followup on all of these comments, particularly on Mr. Shannon's. There's no question that Congress is asserting its role in the government, I think more in recent years than it had in the years prior to the most recent years. But to call this a return to congressional government and to draw an analogy between this period and, say, the 1870's I think is not paying enough attention to the difference in the historical context. Today the Congress in almost every example you can site of its assertiveness is reacting to presidential initiatives, actions taken by the President, to his proposals and so on. In previous eras where we've spoken of congressional assertiveness it has been much more the case that the Congress has been proposing initiatives, ignoring those of the President or, alternatively, in the absence of any initiative taken by the President for whatever reason he has not to take the initiative. I think in terms of the Congress' structure today, also, this decentralized mode of operation which has been in existence for fifty years or is the reason why we need not worry about congressional government. The problem we have to focus on is how we can create a system of government, a legislative-executive system, where Congress does not impede itself or intrude itself excessively into administration.

This raises a question, I think, in terms of how the White House and its decision process should be structured. How can the President structure his decision process so as to enhance the possibility that relations with the Congress will not lead to unfortunate intrusions into administration? I see two different answers to this. One is the whole idea of more open Presidential decisions: turn away from the White House staff, rely on cabinet officers who can go up to the Hill and testify, who have to go up and testify, and try to rebuild comity and trust. I personally don't think that is as effective as another method and that would be to create a system whereby the President can come forth with concisely and persuasively packaged initiatives which can be sold and taken to the Hill where they will garner support. The congressmen aren't ready on their own to create initiatives. They are very ready, if they see one that is put together effectively, to follow it and perhaps tack on a few amendments here and there but not obstruct it. The difficulty is that that system of effective coordination at the presidential level has broken down. The difference between congressional government I think . . .

LYNN: Well, let me give you a golden rule on how to package something that will get ready acceptance in the Congress. If you package a new initiative that involves more money or tax cuts— although since tax cuts are always a threat to spending more money they're more careful about that, because they don't want it to get in the way of the increased spending—you will win, and you will have good liaison. On the other hand, if you want to package anything that's going to cause grief back home in the district, there isn't any genius that you can use other than one—and this shows a quality of a particular presidency—which is to go back home to get to the people of the United States and explain, as President Carter is trying to do at the present time, we tried, too—I think he's doing a quite good job however in this regard—that we do have this crisis, it's a difficult problem, and we have got to address it. But there is your basic problem. The basic problem is for a President to get enough of a consensus of what people will say to their congressmen and what they write in letters that the Congress will respond to their people back home, not the President. And I don't know that there's anything wrong with that, but that's the basic point. No matter how well you package it—whether you do the most beautiful job of charts, graphs, etc., you can consult for twenty weeks with a congressman or a senator, you can take each one of them on one-on-one for thirty months—and it won't do you any good on a tough issue unless you've gone to the people, and the people understand the issue, and that congressman or senator feels secure in voting with you. It's as simple as that.

GOLDWIN: Much of this struggle we've been talking about between Congress and the executive, I suppose, was foreseen by the authors of *The Federalist* who wrote of ambition counteracting ambition and connecting the interests of the man in office with the constitutional rights of the office. That kind of conflict and competition was intended, but it aggravates everybody. When it goes too far one way or the other there is a concern. The thing that I worry about, and I can only sense it—I think those of you who had the kind of experience in the White House that I did not have could speak more knowledgably about this—what I worry about is that now, for a variety of reasons, the bureaucracy can always figure out a way to benefit from the struggle between the executive and the Congress. As a result, bureaucratic projects acquire a life of their own, vast programs that have no traceable legislative basis. I can give you some examples. For instance, the affirmative action program has no legislative basis. It started with an executive order which had no details in it other than the phrase "affirmative action." It got fleshed out by the Labor Department in an order having to do primarily with building contractors who had federal contracts; the details were spelled out in terms of employment practices, promotion practices, and so on. In that Labor order, HEW was delegated to draw up similar regulations for institutions of higher education who were federal contractors. HEW, then, several years later, finished drawing up higher education guidelines which introduced the phrases "numerical goals" and "timetables" for the first time. And that has become identified as the meaning of affirmative action.

Everybody knows now what a massive impact that has had on higher education throughout the country, and now no one can undo it. The President could conceiveably just say, "My executive order is canceled and everything else depending on it is canceled." But imagine the uproar that would cause; it has a life of its own without ever having been through any kind of congressional hearings, deliberations, debates, votes or anything else that usually is the basis for a very large program.

I'll give another example. The Internal Revenue Service has developed a program that applies to all private schools: all private schools are required to show that they have a racially nondiscriminatory policy in hiring of employees and faculty, and in admission of students, as a condition for obtaining or maintaining a tax-exempt certificate. Now, that applies to every private school, from nurseries on up through the highest levels of graduate education. The school doesn't have to be a federal contractor; it applied to every private school, because they all have to have tax exemption to survive. That has no legislative basis and no executive order basis. There was a federal court decision in the state of Mississippi, and it applied only to the state of Mississippi and to states with a similar history of dual school systems. And on that basis, IRS persuaded the counsel of the Treasury and the secretary of the treasury into thinking that they were required by court order to undertake an affirmative action program. It was only after the order was adopted that it became clear there was no court mandate, that the best you could say was that it does not conflict with a court decision that had much narrower scope. Now, any administration would seem to be against racial nondiscrimination if tried to undo it.

So it seems to me that the bureaucracy has acquired a kind of legislating, deliberating, and acting role. I think it has something to do with competition of the executive and legislative branches. And it has to do, too, with the tendency of both to try to increase the size of their staffs to cope with the other. Each time they do increase their staffs, they get more bureaucrats who generate more programs on their own without any real democratic authorization. And so you get larger congressional staffs, larger executive staffs to cope with them, and pretty soon they are doing as much legislating and acting as either the Congress or the people who think of themselves as the administration.

STORING: It also has a lot to do with the point that Herb Stein made about the quantitative increase in the work the government is doing.

STEIN: I think that that's a very important point that Bob Goldwin has just made. But in addition there is a lot of lawmaking going on in the administrative branch and with some legislative authority. That is, Congress passes legislation that gives the administration so much discretion that everybody is making legislation. Then Congress wants to see how that works out. And EPA is a great example. They have legislative authority, but they're affecting everybody's lives in a very discretionary way. Somebody in Congress wants to watch that, but of course those 535 congressmen can't watch it so you get an enormous staff there and you have the bureaucratic government on both sides with the legislation and administration totally confused.

*   *   *

CHENEY: The Congress is very well oriented to producing short-term benefits for long-term hidden costs. They're great at increasing social security benefits levels, more welfare programs, more spending on public service centered jobs, and so forth. They are generally very bad, given their short time horizon, two-year cycles . . .

BESSETTE: Well, half have six-year cycles.

CHENEY: . . . at imposing costs now for long-term benefits that are going to arrive in 1985 or 1990. And one of the institutional problems between the two places is that Presidents to some extent *are* forced to think in those terms and that Congress isn't. . . . (inaudible).

GOLDWIN: It's hard to run for office on the slogan, "Fly later, pay now."

BESSETTE: But none the less, don't Presidents, because they are the center of attention, because they have long-term reputations to worry about, don't they concern themselves with that fact, especially in the second term, say, when they don't have to worry about reelection? What else is there to fight for besides your final reputation?

HENRY: This discussion in the last few minutes raises the question whether we are talking about the most important things. If we are in an era of perception politics, then maybe we ought to shift our thinking and assume that the principle output of the presidency is not correct decisions, like we were talking about this morning, but it's symbols and (inaudible) interpretation. And just conceivably if the apparatus around the President spends an equivalent effort, let's say on things like value analysis, public opinion analysis, dynamics of public opinion, the flexibility of symbols and the compatability of certain symbols with correct policy among certain symbols with not very good policy, maybe that is really the job of the President in the next couple of decades, to some extent supercede but not completely replace the kind of decision analysis exercises that we've been going through and which most of the people around the table were mostly involved with during the Ford administration.

LYNN: Don't let the lack of discussion of the other lead to an assumption that there wasn't one heck of a lot of time spent . . .

HENRY: I'm sure it was, but the question is was that kind of discussion as professional, or as serious, or deep, or systematic as the decision analysis.

. . . (inaudible) . . .

GOLDWIN: When the questions were whether there was going to be enough energy, or whether we'd have troops in the right place, or whether prices would be going up or down, on such matters the deliberations were very professional. As to the questions of how the public would receive decisions and how we ought to describe them to the public, you could tell, and I'm sure they all agree, they were all amateurs.

*   *   *

SCOWCROFT: One argument goes counter to what Joe (Bessette) was saying about the proper roles, consultative as opposed to the operational role, and Congress has, I think engaged itself in the operational role . . .

BESSETTE: I wouldn't deny that.

SCOWCROFT: ... more preeminently than they have in the consultation.

NOLTING: We're inclined to take a perhaps more relaxed viewpoint about this trend towards congressional assertiveness. Wouldn't you think, for example, the War Powers Resolution of 1973, it seems to me that that was a direct reaction to Vietnam.

And it would be probably removed from the books or modified in the direction of the Senate version as time goes on and Vietnam fades in the public memory. It seems to me that it is beginning to swing the other way.

*   *   *

CHENEY: Well, what they do though, they complain if you don't consult; if you *do* consult in advance and get agreement—I'm thinking now of Angola, the situation we had with Angola in the Senate—frequently when the time comes to stand up and be counted, when the decision is criticized, none of them are there. It won't be sort of outright denial that they were involved in the process at all, but they all head for the cloak room when it comes time to stand up and be counted.

SCOWCROFT: Well, I think that was basically true of Vietnam ...

CHENEY: They're totally nonaccountable.

SCOWCROFT: ... which led to the War Powers Act. It was not that the Congress didn't know what was going on in Vietnam, however many games Johnson may have played from time to time. There was vote after vote after vote. Not only about the Tonkin Gulf Resolution but budget after budget where Congress had a chance to weigh in. It was only when it started to become unpopular that the Congress started to bail out. And I think there's inevitably going to be true in this sort of area.

CHENEY: The one thing to mention in line with your caveat not to go without bringing something up—we touched on it previously in a couple of places—as the politics of perception. Someone mentioned our relationship with the fourth estate. There's a whole area there where I think the literature is very weak in terms of the impacts, your communications needs, and your relationship with the press, and how you organize the staff of the White House and what percentage or portion of your resources—not only in terms of bodies but in terms of the percentage of everybody's time—is devoted to basic fundamental communications, press relations, and it is enormous. If you look just at the press office you'd be misled because that's only about ten percent of the White House staff, but that's still a lot, relatively speaking. And the impact of television, the fact that you've got no choice but to communicate through the press whatever it is you're trying to convey to the country to provide leadership—it turns the operation into show business, I guess is the best way to put it. It's important to be able to communicate and convey but so much of our activities and our efforts were just dominated, not with quote, "policy decisions," but with policy decisions with everything wrapped around that and the question of what its impact would be on the public, how it would be percieved, how do we get the nets to cover it, what kind of coverage will they give it, what time of day should we do it, what program are we going to knock off—is it going to be Bonanza, is it going to be Police Woman . . .

LYNN: Or a football game. That's a real bummer.

CHENEY: . . . or a football game. I don't think those things have ever been adequately dealt with in terms of looking at the presidency. There's a tendency to look at the press and talk about First Amendment freedoms and so forth and news management. But the fact of the matter is if you don't try to manage the news and if you don't have an awful lot of resources internally devoted to that question of what the viewers will see on the tube in the evening, there's no way you can begin to be effective in terms of the policies.

LYNN: A conflict I have and partially it's a political conflict in my own mind—I answered a little earlier that you can have the most concisely prepared papers and the best proposals in the world, but if you don't get to the people so they in turn communicate with the Congress you don't have a chance. So one side of that point is to be charismatic, imaginative, and win the press, and win the tube, by way of getting your story across to America. And we can talk about good ways to do that. The problem is to the extent that the executive branch is the focal point for that, rather than if you read the Constitution on the legislation, really initiates on Capitol Hill, it doesn't initiate with the executive branch; when you read it that way—that hasn't been the way for a long while—you are giving an incumbent an enormous tool politically. And I keep saying to myself, I always have one view when my man is in another view when the other fellow is in, which is perfectly human. Is there some way of balancing this off between the two branches in a way that to some extent you can ease my dilemma in this regard? Because the President's opportunity to get his viewpoint across to the people is, as I say, somehow bothersome to me when measured against congressional efforts in this regard. Now, the problem in part is, again, that the process in the legislature is so fractionated there's no way even if a network, or others, or the media, wants to present comparable time on the tube and so on that they can do it or get the ratings if they do it. But that *is* a problem to me, and I have to admit I don't have any solutions to it—which ties in with what you're saying, Dick (Cheney), looked at from the other side.

CHENEY: Yes, there's a tendency to look at the White House and say, o.k., here's the White House and here's the Congress, in relation to the Congress, and there's a sort of a nice neat dividing line there, and much of the debate takes place over who crosses over the dividing line. Maybe the press is a little bit different in the sense that you live with them. They're in the building—it's almost an incestuous relationship— in the bedroom; you get on the airplane and they've got the ten seats in the back end of the aircraft; you go overseas on a foreign trip, there's one plane for the President and his staff and two plane-loads full of press guys. And when it comes time to talk about policy I would argue that—I know the President himself has said this—we often felt we made excellent policy but we were unable to get it across because somehow the communications system broke down. And I can't stress strongly enough the need in my view, to the extent that you have an academic interest in studying the presidency, that whole area is ripe.

STORING: Let me ask a followup. To what extent is an important consideration there—I know this is a delicate subject—the way in which the speechwriting function is intergrated into the rest of what goes on? One has the impression that Presidents have differed a lot in this respect. In some, the speechwriting function is the core of thinking in the White House. In others, it's something that's done at some later point.

CHENEY: Well, in our perspectives, one of the problems we always had, frankly, was trying to integrate the speechwriting process with the policy process. And with the political process. The simplistic view of it would be to say, you sit down, you look at the options paper, you make a decision, and then you write a speech and explain what it is you are going to do. In reality what happens is that oftentimes the speech process ends up driving the policy process. It surfaces when it comes time to sit down and put it on paper and to get the secretary of treasury to agree with the chairman of the CEA and the director of OMB on exactly what that policy decision meant; issues are raised through the process that have to then be resolved by the President and almost becomes an integral part of the policymaking process. Ideally, that's the way it works. And it was a problem for us.

SCOWCROFT: I think it's one of the things we did the least well.

LYNN: It could become in effect a second review of the policy and it can be without as good a system for that review. And many of the finer points that led to the original decisionmaking can get lost in that second review because the speech review process wasn't put together in the way that afforded all those niceties of the system. And that can be a very difficult time.

CHENEY: And a classic example of how you can get harmed, how not to do it, was campaign stuff which we developed and had written: the definitive Ford administration's statement on agriculture policies which was issued during the campaign. And (inaudible) keep it in mind that the vast majority of the American people derived their views on what happened that day on the campaign trail from the evening news. And we were at the University of Iowa. The President stood up, had been through long days of campaigning, and made a very normal slip: he said it's great to be here at the University of Ohio. Of course everybody broke up, roared and laughed and clapped. He corrected himself humorously and went on with it. That night on all three networks the only thing you saw about the coverage ever on television of that speech was the blooper. Not one word about the substance of what he wanted to do in terms of agricultural policy. And you have to live with that. That's the nature of the beast as such that we poured a hell of a lot of time and effort into conveying what he felt was something very important to the American people, a fundamental part of the political process and the electoral process, and what we got was a TV blooper.

*   *   *

STORING: Part of this is, of course, technical. I mean the way the news is summed up. I often think of the Lincoln-Douglas debates where those men were out there and they would talk for three hours in the afternoon, a close, tightly reasoned argument before hundreds of farmers and people who came, then they'd break for dinner, and then another three or four hours in the evening...

CHENEY: CBS would give it thirty seconds. (Laughter)

STORING: Well, CBS would give it thirty seconds assuming we had anyone who could do it.

LYNN: You know the great media put-on that says, "Moses came down with the Ten Commandments today, the two most important of which were..." (Laughter)

RHOADS: Actually, Herb (Storing), you raised just the subject I had in mind; you know, the talk that we made good decisions but we couldn't get them across. And immediately everybody thinks that the problem must have been with our press relations. It would be interesting to kind of explore in more detail what you think *they* were. But the one thing the President can control absolutely is what he says. I wonder if there isn't a connection perhaps between the one substantive problem you saw with the President, inability to kind of take a broad conceptual view, and the fact that there weren't any kind of big memorable speeches which the news media would have to react to, a new view of government or something that they just couldn't avoid.

CHENEY: Our communications problem was not just a press problem. I think that would be an inaccurate statement.

RHOADS: Then was it just the inarticulateness of the President? Was it also the fact that . . .

GOLDWIN: It's something deeper, I think, and it has to do with the state of political rhetoric, understanding what it is and what its function ought to be. There is a notion that whenever anything has to be written in the White House you have to have a writer. And there were people who were there because they were thought to have a facility for writing, and no other known talent or reason for being there. On the other side of it, none of the leading persons in the White House thought of themselves as writers, although many of them when pressed—when some statement was required on short notice and something had to be hammered out—turned out to be as good as the ones who were thought of as writers. Now, that disjunction of the ones who were thought to have a high level of judgment and of respon-sibility, on the one hand, and the ones who were asked to do the writing, on the other hand, is, if not the root problem, a clear symptom of what the problem is. Unless political people at the highest levels feel that a part of their training and responsibility, as they rise to high levels of office, should include writing of their own and other people's public utterances, we will not have a better level of political dis-course.

CHENEY: I think you've got to be a little bit careful here to distinguish between communications very broadly defined and the written word or the, quote, "speech." We spent an awful lot of time finding ways to communicate besides when he stands up and gives a speech. We had problems sometimes with the speeches. Sometimes we had great speeches, when he was sworn in and the Kansas City acceptance address. On other occasions we would do other things like the budget briefing he did, January 1976. It was just a masterful piece. It wasn't the country at large so much as it was directed directly to the Washington press corps. At that point it totally put to rest the whole question we then were faced with politically which is the bungler, stumbler, hit-your-head-on-the-helicopter type image. We did it very deliberately.

GOLDWIN: That budget briefing is an example of what I think one could strive for, and that is a President, through long practice (which was what he was displaying in the budget briefing), capable of expressing himself in his own words at the highest level on major issues.

STEIN: I'd also like to say something else about the interaction between speeches and policies. It's not only that making a speech provides the occasion for articulating a policy that has been agreed upon. It is often the occasion for forcing the development of a policy. That is, you know that the President has to make a speech every once in a while. He can't make a speech unless he says something. You cannot consider that he says somethings these days unless it's a program for spending a billion dollars. This gentleman said, well, was the President unable, was the President's difficulty in communicating the result of something in his technique or because he didn't have any new philosophy of government to convey? I think that's very typical. If he had a new philosophy of government to convey, he would have gotten on at prime time. But suppose he just wanted to convey his devotion to the old philosophy, and it's a very good old philosophy, and a very good old-time religion economics. That doesn't sell.

LYNN: It's not news.

CHENEY: It isn't innovative.

STEIN: So the media drives the character of policy in activist, dramatic, zig-zag direction. There are many speeches I remember when first it was decided to have a speech on a certain date and then it was said, well, now what will our policy be to, you know, pump this up? And that's not a good way to make policy.

CONNOR: I think that Herb (Stein) is alluding to something here that ought to be explored in an awful lot of detail. We had experience with it; Carter is having it now. It is the way in which decisions are made or in which symbols are cast in order to achieve what the President needs in terms of conveying his general message. I need to get time on the nets. I need to get a headline. Because if I don't do that, if I come out with something that makes a reasonable amount of sense and is issued as a statement, it clearly will not appear on the nets, it appears in a relatively few newspapers and then generally back with truss ads. And then you are asked, why hasn't he done anything about this? The Ford administration—every administration—has had the frustration of being accused of not doing anything on important issues. You say, well, we did the following things back then. The funniest reaction is from the guy in the press you tell that to. He says, well, we didn't know about it. If the fact that they didn't know, that it wasn't cast in the kind of a setting which would ring all their bells, was our fundamental problem—now it may be a fundamental problem—but if that is the case, then I think everybody has to start thinking very carefully of the implications of that. If the only things that become facts are things which are elaborated in a certain kind of way, then you find yourself with a definition of government that gets kind of scary.

LYNN: Let me give you a bet as to what is going on right now. The commitment has been made that by May 1 all of the energy legislation will be delivered to the Congress of the United States. Now there's a commitment that's been made. But unless Jim Schlesinger and his three guys have been writing it all in his own department without any interagency coordination, they won't meet the schedule. They haven't begun yet to have any kind of a coordinated approach to flushing out those broad proposals. One example is the proposal that every person that gets utility services will now have a loan program from his friendly utility company to pay for a retrofit on all his energy-related equipment, and in turn the utility will have the power to go to Fanny Mae or Freddie Mac and get the money from the market through the Federal system. There is a set of subissues in there that is absolutely enormous. Now, the President said he's going to have the legislation by May 1, and his instinct is absolutely right. The Hollywood side of it is to keep that movement going, get something new to the press so that they will not say, well, that was yesterday's news and incidently Amy's putting a roof on her treehouse. (Laughter) And to get that, he's got to keep that momentum going. But these decisions are things that ought to be taking appreciable time. And that's just the best example I can come up with currently as to what I think is happening (inaudible).

Or it may make sense for the President to go to XYZ University. It is the right time to do that, so now let's do something on education. It may not be the right time, in a substantive priority sense, to do education, but the scheduling process controls. He's going to be at that institute of higher education, so now the whole process will go to work to come up with something in the higher education field. And then cabinet officers salivate and say, "Three new programs, that's what we need." And you've got to fight that.

BESSETTE: I had a couple of questions on the apparent drive to communicate something on every issue. What is the reason for the drive? Is is basically electoral, or does it have to do with generating public support that then gets back to Congress with policies?

LYNN: Both.

BESSETTE: Do you get more backing for the legislative program by going over the heads of Congress?

LYNN: You've got it. You've got it.

BESSETTE: But the other side of that is that you had a Republican President and a Democratic Congress, which meant that some of the usual mechanisms for getting a program through were not there.

LYNN: A congressman or a senator will buy the program if he thinks either a) it will help back home or b) it will not be decisive in his losing back home. To get to the second one you may, on one-on-one with him, convince him. But if he is in doubt as to whether it can be really material the next time around, you can sit with him for twenty months and it won't make any difference. You can get a little crass and there may be something he wants more, too, and he'll take a chance because you gave him something else. But in the main when you get to that kind of issue—energy—when you get to the split-personality-of-the-American-people issues—like they want to have spending cut down, they want taxes reduced, they want inflation under control, on the one hand, but they also want their favorite program, you know, don't do as I do but do as I tell you kind of thing—if you're trying to sell as President Ford was in October of 1974—I am going to balance the budget within three years; I am going to slow the growth of federal spending to thus and so; and this is going to be tough to do; and I'm going to cut taxes—the only way you're really going to carry out that policy, and it's going to take time to do it, is to hammer that home to the American people.

CHENEY: We found during the campaign that their information circuits are overloaded most of the time. And from the standpoint of political leadership from the presidency, and I don't want to put a value on what they have got stored in their heads, but a lot of it's useless and their attention span is very short.

We found during the campaign that the President had taken a position consistently, well over a year, for tax cuts—we had tax legislation pending on the Hill, and we had special messages and addresses to the Congress, and so on and so forth, it went on and on and on and on. And in October just before the election you'd still get poll results back that fifty percent of the American people didn't know he was for tax cuts, didn't know what his position was on taxes. You know, and you'd literally broken your back to convey that very basic fundamental message that a voter ought to care about. In this day and age given all the other stuff that's impinging on the private citizen, whose attention you want to get, and you're competing with Mary Hartman and whatever else you've got to worry about, you can only get him for maybe thirty seconds a night on the evening news, and he's probably going to see that maybe twice a week. And you end up to some extent really screwing the message all out of shape just to get that thirty second segment in.

STORING: Yes, that's worrisome.

CHENEY: But it's a fact.

STORING: Well, facts are very often worrisome.

LYNN: If you'd sit down with Jody Powell he'd tell you, I'm sure if he told it, too, straight up, that that is exactly what they're coping with, but in my judgment are handling quite well.

STORING: One of the things I think we might sometime do is a study of presidential rhetoric because characteristically, although Nixon was an exception and maybe to some extent Ford, presidential rhetoric these days is a series of one sentence paragraphs, no one of which is connected in any rational way with one that precedes it or follows it.

LYNN: Because each one can be a twelve second segment.

STORING: That's right, exactly.

CONNOR: That's why you write them that way.

STORING: Well, I'm not sure because I think . . .

CONNOR: That *is* why you write them that way, let me tell you. You don't write a thirty-eight word sentence that is nicely balanced to convey a complex idea, because they are going to take some segment of that. They're going to take nine of the words and you don't know which nine they're going to take. So you get very good at . . .

STORING: Yes, although one might make an argument, one might respond to this, I admit, absolutely massive concern by wondering whether there isn't a preoccupation with only one piece of your audience or your news media, namely that TV network, and whether there isn't in fact another, or a whole lot of other audiences, for example, that very small but conceivably influential group of people who might read a reasoned statement, and who might in turn influence other people.

. . . (inaudible) . . .

CONNOR: I was just going to say that there are two dangers that you face with the perception politics. It's obvious what danger you face if you don't do it well; you don't get elected. The danger you face if you do it well and continue to do it, is what *are* we really conveying, what are those images? We may convey a favorable image, but is that not a part of the process of raising expectations which can only be dashed? I think that as a society we've got to be very concerned about the way in which that leads. What occurs as we move more and more toward less substantive ideas away from a three hour debate in which you may only understand part of it, but you know they said this and they said that—to a quick notion of strength, warm, puppy dog feelings, you name it? There are things that the political system may be trying to convey to people which it can never deliver. And so we've put ourselves in a kind of manic-depressive situation. We become elated, but the *way* in which we become elated—that's right—we go through our manic phase and what causes the manic phase can only lead to a depressive phase thereafter.

GOLDWIN: That goes back to Herb Stein's argument, that that kind of politicking is most inappropriate for the person who refuses to offer wild new programs of multi-billion dollar spending—so, if your message is a conservative one, the medium is all wrong.

CONNOR: I'm not sure. Here's where I think Carter is going to be very interesting to watch. Because what Carter may be doing is playing a very big gamble on conveying his set of expectations, which *are* brand-new, bold, etc., but in terms of the actions being taken, not particularly brand-new or bold. It's going to be a very interesting kind of game to see. Maybe he can play a quasi-conservative presidency in fiscal terms with very liberal rhetoric, I think (inaudible).

STEIN: I just wanted to insert the notion that there are motivations for presidential speeches other than political—everything is political—but I think there are occasions when he is speaking not in an attempt to get any support for himself or for legislation of Congress, but to have an effect on the country. And I think mainly of a number of economic speeches where the President thought that he could have some effect on the behavior of the private economy by his speeches, especially by creating confidence—that is the general term—to explain the situation to the country, to explain what he is doing, not with the intention of asking for any support, but just to kind of calm down the country. And I think a lot of those early Vietnam speeches were of that character in '69 and '70, to, maybe get the students out of Lafayette Park, just to settle things down. There are motives for communication other than what might seem the more instrumental ones. I think you were right in saying that maybe we have been exaggerating with this nine word segment on TV. Mr. Nixon certainly thought there was an big audience out there of people sitting on tractors listening to the radio, and he liked to talk to them at noon.

CHENEY: I don't want to beat the subject to death, but on the question of playing to television vs. other media forms, the fact of the matter is there are two or three newspapers that do a good job of covering the White House in terms of fairly detailed coverage, highly competent people who are very professional and experienced in the business. You're talking about the *New York Times* and the *Washington Post* and maybe one or two others, *The Wall Street Journal* sometimes. A handfull of people. The other two things you're left with are the wire services which tend to dominate what goes into most (inaudible) throughout the country and television. You try to cover everybody when you do an event. You try to have a detailed fact sheet or prepare a prereleased text that the *New York Times* can print in its entirety. But when the man stands up to do it, you're worried about the background, camera angles, and what segment of it is going to come out in the news. If you got yourself locked into the situation where you didn't give sufficient attention to television and to the nine word segment, you'd get (inaudible) in terms of trying to convey anything to the country, because you can get the opinion leaders but Joe Sixpack is never going to get the message.

STORING: Gentlemen, we're at 4:30 and I didn't give you a break. I suggest you think of delivering yourself of your final thoughts.

CONNOR: In thinking about the Ford presidency you've got to be very cautious—all of us, those who were parts of it and those looking at. Dick Neustadt said you can really only judge a presidency in its third, fifth, and six years. The reason he says this is because it's learning what the hell it's all about, how to do things, in the first two. You've got a third year where it's shaken down. The fourth year's out because you're in the middle of an election. The fifth and sixth, you've won the election presumably and you're going ahead. Seventh and eighth, lame duck, everybody is starting to discount you, thinking about what's going on next. The Ford administration in its last year was simultaneously in its second and fourth year. It was never in a third and fifth year. I think those of us who were inside began to see it shake down as it went along. We never saw what that third and fifth and sixth years would be. And it's very hard to make a judgment of it. I think we all should be cautious about it.

GOLDWIN: I'm not sure if Neustadt's right on how you should judge a President, though. My family used to be in the restaurant business. And restaurants always have rush hours and slow hours. The test of a restaurant is how it performs in the rush hour under the greatest strain. It's easy to be good when there is no pressure. But when everybody is overworked and rushed, that's when you should be judged. Neustadt picked the years when, as the saying goes, you can be a statesman, not a politician. I think the test of an administration is how it performs under the greatest pressure.

CONNOR: I think what he's saying is that, first there is a period of learning and shaking down in an administration that goes well beyond one hundred days, or six months, or whatever.

GOLDWIN: Well, one of the tests for Presidents is how they perform in the shake-down period. Every administration seems to have a great crisis early, and they must handle that. Every administration knows, at least since the Bay of Pigs, that in the first few months they had better be on guard, because something horrendous is going to occur, something that's a test.

CHENEY: The WIN program. (Laughter)

DAVID: I'd like to comment in terms of this conversation that's just been going, that I think that much of what is going on today, especially the remarks of the last few minutes, relates to what might be called life cycle theory. Every administration has a life cycle which it goes through, a series of repetitive events that will go with the calendar, the election calendar in particular, but also the budget calendar, the message calendar, and all the rest. As far as I know, no one has ever written an article on life cycle theory. I've delivered a lecture on it every year for the last several years with one page of notes. But it does seem to me that this is a subject that could lend itself to being rather specifically exploited in ways that as far as I know never have been. I think the remarks of Dick Neustadt are very much in point, but he's never written them up that way.

SCOWCROFT: Well, we haven't really had a standard one since Eisenhower, in terms of the constitutional presidential term.

DAVID: Well, Nixon's first term, he had a full four years.

SCOWCROFT: No, I'm thinking of an eight year cycle where you go through the first building four years, and through the lame duck ...

CAVANAUGH: Through five or six or whatever.

STORING: Further comments, gentlemen?

CEASER: I just had one final comment (inaudible) on the Ford staff, the point that Hess brings up: incoming staff is so heavily influenced and recruited by the President's election campaign, and that this staff was so differently formed. I think as a consequence there is a different sort of person who related to the President in a different way, and it seems to me an altogether healthier one, than the staff which is formed out of the presidential campaign. And I had some worries about that.

NOLTING: Herbert, one thing I think hasn't been discussed and probably there is not time to discuss it is the influence and importance of the federal judiciary on the President and particularly the Supreme Court in its decisions, and the direction in which they move towards, in the last five or six years, towards more assertive action, not only in terms of decision but in terms of attempts to run schools, and prisons, and other things of that sort. I just flag that because it's an important part of this which we haven't touched.

STORING: Both in respect to participation in active administration, and also of course with respect to the presidency itself.

STEIN: I'd like to generalize the point that Mr. Ceaser made about looking at the people and the qualities, the qualifications of staff people and whether it is possible to predict and select who will be useful staff people. Because I remember first coming into the White House and seeing all these advance men and ad men and so on. But many of them turn out to be very able people. But it would not have been predictable, it seems to me, and I think most academics would have thought what I thought. And I think that's a subject—what is it that makes a good staff person is worth some investigation.

STORING: The answer may be very simple: you can't tell.

STEIN: Yes, maybe so.

HENRY: Another constitutional query: Does the Ford-Rockefeller experience prove once again the old historical adage that even with the best intentions no useful work can be found for the vice-president?

CONNOR: Yes. (Laughter)

...(inaudible)...

CHENEY: That was a fascinating relationship to watch develop. And I would have to say that we did try exceedingly hard to carve out a substantial area of responsibility for the vice-president. The President and vice-president, in spite of some difficulties that developed structurally in terms of how that worked between the two of them—there was at the end of their time in office a much closer and warmer relationship than between any two other people in the administration. But institutionally I would have to agree with Jim (Connor). The problem when you try to put a vice-president in roles, you're always trying to fit him somehow in staff operations inside the White House. And the fact of the matter is you've got a different set of criteria for selecting a vice-president than you do staff. And by virtue of the fact that he is a constitutional officer, that he isn't subject to the same kinds of—that it's a different relationship, that other staff people oftentimes will defer to him as vice-president, rather than treat him as a staff person and argue and debate with him and so forth. There are just some very basic fundamental problems there in trying to make that work.

CONNOR: And the only other alternative you've got for him is some kind of a line position, and it seems to me you've got your lines pretty well filled. You have cabinet officers—there has been considerable discussion about them—they by and large have the line responsibilities. And every one of them is entitled by virtue of the piece of paper on his wall to appeal directly to the President and not to go through a line of someone else in the system.

LYNN: But the way your question was put, I have to put it this way. I think you are fortunate if you can have a vice-president, given all the factors that surround that choice, who is substantially younger than you are who is not posed as a present threat to you, and you're running a second time. And if that person has a particular area of expertise or background that is important to you, as long as you do not make the error of formalizing what those areas are of that person, that is the place where having somebody that is a free agent and able to come in and talk is useful. I think a vice-president can be very useful. And the more useful he is, the less the press will be able to pin him down how he was being useful. But he has a vested interest in the success of this President because he sees himself trying to run on it in eight years. On the other hand, he does have his own problems. He might want, as the administration may go sour, to have some distance between the President and him. The more quiet that fellow is, the more there is some room, fireworks go off. But a good vice-president can be eyes and ears to hear what's going on, and maybe, like a management consultant has as his greatest advantage, he doesn't know that much about every subject and therefore can ask a question that fundamentally may seem stupid to the people who've been immersed in the subject, but it may be exactly the right question to ask.

GOLDWIN: Why didn't the announced plan work for Nelson Rockefeller to be the head of the Domestic Council?

LYNN: Because you should never never let your President and, in my own judgment, your vice-president, get in that kind of position where as they're digging for the stories as to who killed Cock Robin, who was on each side of the issue, who got support—did the vice-president win or lose?

CHENEY: You can afford to have a staff member lose.

LYNN: That's right, but never put the vice-president in a position where he . . .

GOLDWIN: Is that why it didn't work?

CHENEY: It's just one of several reasons. You simply can't paint it in simply totally black and white terms, that it worked or didn't work. I don't quite know how to say it, but it's a matter of, if you believe in the staff system the way most of us talked about it today, which is a structure, and the idea of the give and take of ideas, and an idea that goes into that system has to get shot at by its enemies and its opponents—taking a man or woman who's vice-president of the United States and putting him into that has an impact not only on them, in terms of whatever advice they may give, but it also has an impact on the others in process because they react to the vice-president very differently than they do to the director of OMB or their colleagues on the staff. And the other thing I'd have to say is, if the vice-president has a very general, vague kind of thing like Jim (Lynn) is talking about, it's easy to forget about him when it's time to sit down and solve a problem. If there's a foreign policy crisis, you know you've got to have the secretary of state, secretary of defense, and the head of the NSC there. If you have a budget problem, you want Lynn. If you have an HEW problem, you want the guy from HEW. But the vice-president doesn't automatically fit into any one of these responsibilities. He's got to be a floater. And once you're a floater then the extent to which people automatically bring you in rely upon you and use you is different.

CONNOR: There's plenty of room for relatively low-level floaters in the system, people who can move from problem to problem, can get into fights and arguments and can afford to lose arguments. A high-level floater in the system, a super-high level, which is the vice-president, that doesn't fit into the system.

SCOWCROFT: I think in the sense that the question was asked the answer has got to be negative. However useful the relationship can be, I think in the sense that you ask the question, it appears to us to be negative. Although I think fairly we have to say that the present administration is trying very hard and in a somewhat different way to make it work.

CHENEY: Mondale has got a unique set of qualifications in the sense that—this is just my own view from the outside—that he's the resident expert on the Hill. The people that Carter brought with him that are close in his personal staff have no knowledge of the Hill. Even the guy who runs congressional relations has no knowledge of the Hill except what he has acquired since getting in the job. And the vice-president now currently is able to be enormously helpful in managing congressional relations in a sense in a way that is due to this very special circumstances . . .

LYNN: But it is the kind of thing where your advice can be given quietly to the President, where you don't have to be in a win-lose relationship, because it can go to strategy and tactics which in and of themselves aren't necessarily news—like, Mr. President, I think before you do that you ought to call Mr. X.

CAVANAUGH: Well, that goes back exactly to the point that Dick (Cheney) made earlier that when you have a national security problem you call for the secretary of state and your NSC man. What they're facing now is when they have a congressional problem they only have one man to call on who knows it and that's the vice-president. So they're calling on him.

CHENEY: They need him. He's the best in the building on the subject.

SCROWCROFT: As a matter of fact, he's one of the most expert in government, not just congressional relations.

DAVID: The Mondale thing reminds me of a question I've had in mind during the day as a result of reading the Hess book. The last part of the book of course is heavily on describing, trying to make the presidency more collegial by using the cabinet, with no reference whatever of the leadership meetings with Congress, what I always have assumed were collegial, at least they are a bunch of people that the President can't fire, that he's under some constitutional compulsion now to see once a week when Congress is in session, which has been going on since 1937 as a habit. Nevertheless, somehow they don't seem to be taken very importantly in the literature. We once had a doctoral candidate here who did a doctoral dissertation on the leadership meetings, at least that was what we tried to get him to do. He spent a year in Washington during which he did a good deal of interviewing. But we had great trouble keeping him on the track. Apparently everybody told him they weren't very important and shouldn't be studied much.

CEASER: All the more reason for his dissertation. (Laughter)

LYNN: I think you'll find that a good deal can depend today on who the particular leadership is, because there again the media comes into this. After every leadership meeting out on the lawn the camera is set up and so is the radio, and the people in the leadership have no opportunity to digest what they've heard, to really get ready, or to not skewer the President's position even if they're inclined not to skewer it.

And we have opposite parties, of course. There can be at least a little tilting because of that. And also the view of the leadership toward that President: is he someone we can trust in this meeting to have a frank discussion and that neither side is going to go out either deliberately or, more likely, in a perfectly innocent way and say something that was intended to be kept confidential in that meeting? And I've been to some meetings of the leadership where they have been quite useful, I thought. And they tended to be smaller rather than larger. The less staff sitting around the room . . .

CHENEY: Wouldn't you agree, Jim (Lynn), that one of our problems was that to some extent the concept of leadership was weak? That is to say that oftentimes we'd call the leadership in with the expectation that we would be able to reach an agreement. More often than not we were trying to persuade them to see things our way, agree to support such and such, or to get a bill out, or whatever it might be. But oftentimes they weren't in a position to even give us a definitive response at all because they weren't—and I don't mean this to refer necessarily to the individuals—but they weren't strong leaders.

SCOWCROFT: Well, I think this new phenomenon is one which needs to be investigated and that is that the congressional leadership is a far cry from the Sam Rayburn-Lyndon Johnson kind of leadership, both in each house itself and within the committees. Each chairman is now looking back over his shoulder to see whether or not he's going to be voted out. This is something very new, I think.

CAVANAUGH: That's a phenomenon that we all saw during the Ford presidency: the Democratic caucus and in its emergence; the committee chairman who once could make a commitment and keep it, no longer can do that.

SCOWCROFT: They cannot deliver any more.

LYNN: That's why as I said earlier, although I realize it has certain pie-in-the-sky aspects to it, that unless they can come up with some kind of an umbrella task force committee kind of idea that does not represent a permanent threat either to the leadership as we state it on the masthead or the committee people—although it may be a terrible diminution of their authority on that particular set of issues—there isn't any way that we can know where to go to get anything done, or that President Carter knows where to get it done. That's why the energy umbrella, as I say, is so very important. I remember when President Ford came out with his comprehensive energy package in January of 1975. And I would dare to say it was at least as comprehensive as the one we've just seen from the Carter administration from the standpoint of all things that it touched upon and dealt with. We dealt with things in some areas quite differently and other areas the same. I remember the frustration of sitting there with the leadership where they were talking about getting back to us with their views. And they never got back to us. It became perfectly obvious to them when they went back to the Hill there was no way they could organize it.

CAVANAUGH: They had no mechanism to deal with it. It was a very comprehensive program.

. . . (inaudible) . . .

LYNN: They said, "All we want is sixty days, Mr. President," and there was even a little negotiation on how many days. And I could see looking at other people's eyes around there, they didn't want to get pinned down to any date. And we're trying to give a signal to John Rhodes to get off of that sixty day bit.

NOLTING: What sort of congressional action would be acquired for that umbrella thing?

LYNN: They just do it by their own rules. He's already announced it and he's already appointed Lud Ashley and John Anderson.

CHENEY: It's not done to help the President, basically it's done to give O'Neill great flexibility.

LYNN: It gives him a process to be able to exercise some control, but it does another thing politically. Tip senses, I believe, they can't afford to have Carter in position of saying that we're in a total disarray because we didn't do anything. And yet Tip thinks, and I agree with him, this is the only conceivable way that has any chance of succeeding—of not being put in what politically vulnerable position. So it's enhancing his leadership, yes, but that, if you look at it just in the public interest, is absolutely essential to getting anything done.

STORING: We will make note of these questions that have been put, and record them and convene you again in a year's time, and give you the answers to all of them. (Laughter)

At some points in the conversation one wonders how on earth the American government system works at all, and why it does such a reasonably good job, as in fact it does, given all the problems that seem to be built into it. And part of the answer, I think it is fair to say, is reflecting what Fritz (Nolting) said in opening the session, is the quality of an awful lot of the people who work in it, including many of those sitting around this table. I thank you very much for your participation. I found it extremely illuminating and helpful. I hope others of you have too.